©2019

ISBN 978-1-098-31-630-3

A LEGACY OF

EASTLAND COUNTY
TODAY

The Local News Source

215 S. Seaman St., Eastland, TX 76448
ecn@att.net
eastlandcountytoday@gmail.com

Where individual copies and Association orders are available.

To Gaynell O'Brien
partner in business and life.

Thanks to: Vanessa Clement and the late Ladonna Clement, through many proofs; Sheila Hickox, for advice and assistance; Margaret Hetrick and Mrs. Al (Jan) Novak, who found misspelled words, duplications and made many important recommendations; the late Patrick Ready for encouragement; the entire staff for abiding this folly; and to Vance and Amy, and Jon, and grandchildren Levi, Luke, Laura Leigh and Leigha, who lived through much of the story and always believed in Papa and thought he hung the moon. Special thanks to Linda Spetter, proof reader; and the late J.W. Sitton, Publisher who was employer and motivator.

* * *

A Borrowed Creed:
To comfort
The afflicted
And to afflict
The comfortable

Luke 8:19 (KJV)
"Then came to him his mother and his brethren, and could not come at him for the press."

"There is no shame in not knowing; the shames lies in not finding out!" --Russian Proverb

Table of contents

Chapter 1................................Who stole the pickup?

Chapter 2...Basic training

Chapter 3........................The White House basement

Chapter 4.......................................A lifetime partner

Chapter 5.....................Early editing at the Telegram

Chapter 6................................People I have known

Chapter 7...The High times

Chapter 8..The Low times

Epilogue.............What does it mean to be an Editor?

Appendix........An inside look at Eastland County Newspapers

PREFACE

Why this book? To let others know that it can happen, "even unto the least of these."

It is also written to pass on what I have learned in a lifetime of journalism: patience, honesty, a willingness to work long hard hours, the wish to be fair to all recognizing that all, have flaws and good qualities.

I have dreamed for years that such a book might be valuable, and then one day I realized I might be the one to do it. I believe my route, though sometimes stumbling, was providentially led. And for that reason, I hope this book might help others along the way.

It was June, 1944, in a Baptist tabernacle revival in Carbon, a small town in Central Texas, that I turned my life over to Christ, who accepted me with the promise that He would never forsake me. He didn't promise that it would be easy, and it hasn't been, but He never left me.

In October, 1944, my Daddy, Hous O'Brien, Sr., was killed in an automobile accident. My mother, who never worked outside the home, and I, age 12, had to be the bread winners.

I worked after school on days and weekends at John's Cafe in Carbon, Texas as dishwasher and general flunky. Mother found work. I graduated at 16.

It hasn't been easy, but the Savior has seen us through tough times and good times along the way.

+ + +

You'll read about Viola Payne here later. She was one of our older, but most talented writers, and she must have told me a dozen times, "Oh, how I wish I had gotten into this newspaper business when I was young." She loved it.

CHAPTER 1
Who Stole the Pickup?

Sheriff Lefty Sublett didn't crack a smile when he came into the Telegram newspaper office, "Onus, I've got a warrant for your new editor."

Publisher Onus Dick didn't smile either when he replied, "Lefty, this is his first week on the job. What did he do? He just got back from Ranger."

The nervous new editor a door away trembled and wondered what he had gotten himself and his new wife into.

It was Tuesday after Labor Day, 1961. The editor and his wife of one year had spent most of the holiday weekend unpacking boxes and trying to make an old 1919 two-story house into their new home in Eastland, Texas. He had covered a golf tourney, his first, at Lone Cedar Country Club. The town was ten miles north of the editor's hometown of Carbon where he had grown up.

"He stole Mr. Hodge's pickup," the sheriff explained.

Onus said, "Editor, come in here and tell us what vehicle you took to Ranger."

"You told me the keys were in that old white pickup out front. I took it," the young editor replied.

The Telegram copy was taken to be printed in Ranger, ten miles east on Hwy. 80 in the plant jointly owned by Publishers Dick and Joe Dennis. The Editor had hired at $110.00 a week.

"You took the wrong pickup," the sheriff said. "You took Mr. Hodge's pickup; he also leaves his keys in his old white pickup."

1

As it turned out, a page ad in the Telegram would not have brought any more publicity to the new editor than did my short, comic "brighty" in the next edition honestly detailing that miscue. For years everybody knew me as the pickup thief.

The trail that brought the couple to this county seat town was long and winding and would eventually lead to working in the White House.

In order to go to college, I had taken a job in a newspaper office in Cisco (ten miles west of Eastland on Hwy. 80) and attended Cisco Junior College. Publisher J.W. Sitton recognized that this young greenhorn needed to learn a trade if he was ever to amount to anything.

Learning a Skill

My primary duties in that first job were sweeping out the hot metal plant, helping catch the papers from the old 8-page flatbed duplex press and counting out routes for the dozen or so teen and pre-teen carrier boys. The biggest task was keeping the youngsters corralled in the area where they were supposed to stay to fold their papers for throwing to subscribers. I too had delivered Fort Worth Star Telegrams while in public school.

The Cisco Press was printed Tuesday and Thursday for afternoon delivery and Saturdays for early Sunday-morning delivery. The Printer's Devil was expected to go to the Press office by 5 a.m. on Sunday to distribute the papers to the carriers for their bicycle routes.

The publisher one day sat the beginner down at the Linotype machine and after many scalding molten lead "squirts" and innumerable "pi'ed" (printer's term

2

for "dropped") mats and trays of type, the youngster began to get the hang of it. I obviously had eye-hand coordination.

After junior college, the publisher, a UT graduate, attempted to get the youngster a job at the Daily Texan newspaper in Austin for UT there, but there were no openings, so they went looking in other directions.

The Abilene Reporter-News, then a major Harte-Hanks chain regional paper in Abilene, 50 miles further west on U.S. 80, took him on although they did not have a Linotype opening, and he enrolled in the Baptist school, Hardin-Simmons University for a Journalism degree.

Working for a Daily

I started in the circulation department handling starts, stops and solving "kicks" (missed papers). Later an opening came up in the tape-punching room on the second floor next to the editorial department. There typists operated Teletype machines which punched six-row coded holes in a half-inch wide strip of paper tape to be placed on Linotype machines, which had been upgraded to read the codes and set the slugs of type automatically without hands-on operators. The tape punchers had to learn to read codes in order to know where they were in an article. They worked cheaper than certified Linotype straight-matter machines because without an operator at the machine, there were many foul-ups.

The Associated Press copy came in on Teletype hard copy and on pre-punched tape and the editorial employees had to match copy to tape, and like anything mechanical, anything that could go wrong, did. So there was pandemonium when the phone circuits went down or out and copy had to be hand set or worse, scraped.

The Reporter was printing a morning and evening paper back then, and the day shift didn't have much time to get papers on the street.

Now an Operator

Linotype openings came open, first on the correction machine where lines were re-set after the proof readers had unscrambled the printed messes that the automatic machines made. New hires started on the night shift.

Nimble hands and a calm head were required. Later that nimbleness elevated me up to the agate machine on which all baseball box scores were manually tabulated and set, requiring even more thoughtful attention to detail, as the lines had to be split with a team to each side in a single column, the split slug then were joined together. The top-of-the-line Linotype machines had power saws that severed the slugs, and automatic justifying modes which centered, and moved left or right as needed. The operator had to be on his toes, and it was not unlike juggling four balls at one time due to the small type and need for justifying columns line for line. Shop foreman Bill Maroney did a good job of taking care of his Ace typesetter. Few survived the Agate Machine.

The Korean War had reared its ugly head, and Mrs. Jewell Reeves, the kind, understanding draft board lady at the county seat in Eastland, had permitted the student-printer to graduate with a B.A. in Journalism before moving his name to the top of the list for induction.

4

One-A

He got a diploma at graduation in a mosquito-infested H-SU athletic field.

He worked through the holidays and the shop gave him a going- away event with a little flash camera; one joker told him they had tested all the bulbs.

All expected him to wind up in Korea.

And that's just the beginning.

About Keyboards

You've got to love keyboards to tackle the toughest of all, the 90-key Mergenthaler Linotype contraptions which turned text into printing surfaces. These devices were often referred to as the "e, t, a, o, i, n" machine because those most-used letters are at the extreme left, vertical next to the space bar, also vertical and operated with the left hand. All lower case letters were on the left, and all caps on the right, with punctuation and numbers in order in the middle. These are rarely used now since computers came in.

Next up: best described as a Teletype tape-punching device. Standard keyboard BUT no screen, no vision. The device mechanically punches coded combinations of holes in the three holes above and three holes below with various combinations of holes representing certain letters and/or characters. A center line of small holes pull the tape through and the tape is eventually rolled and put on an automatic reader on typesetting machines to do the same thing that typesetters would do at higher salaries.

And then came word processors; standard keyboards recording data on magnetic discs which when programmed turn out printed hard copy, either by way of daisy wheel strike-ons or electronic impulse coding against carbon ribbons. This is pretty much where this typist is embedded today. The high-speed computer typesetters wish that they could convert one and all to their system so they wouldn't have to re-keyboard stories and articles.

And it all started in Carbon, so an assortment of keyboards have put groceries on tables for many years.

Without a Care

Growing up in the Central Texas village of Carbon was utopia for youth. State Highway 6 ran through it then (now, around); there were no traffic lights and few stop signs. It was the sort of place where tow-headed teens, male and female, played stick ball and kick the can in the streets without fear of being run over.

The boys camped out on vacant lots or in nearby woods, built camp fires, cooked out and slept in rolled-up blankets or on cots if they had access. There was a lot of Boy Scout and Indian "culture" games, reenactments and lots and lots of horse play.

WWII Ends

It's probably where many learned the nasty habit of smoking tobacco, usually from roll-your-own sacks, and often even cedar bark. Chewing recently-poured paving tar was also a foul but not the worst undertaking. But no pot.

As only youth can find ways to entertain themselves and others, one lad in particular named Byron, could with proper or improper gyrations, and much force of internal organs, work up and generate farts much

6

to the delight of all. Unlike Alexander Solzhenitsyn's Gulag, we hadn't learned to hold a match for a streak of fire. Others had many other rare talents which we demonstrated.

We carried slingshots (then known by a different name); some had much-coveted air rifles, and generally we wore shoes only when it was really cold.

Poor? In material things, yes. In the ability to entertain ourselves, rich, with bottles for target practice, Prince Albert cans for carrying precious cargo, and rusty pocketknives which were used for many tasks.

We threw rocks, clods, pears, horse apples and forked sticks at each other in mock warfare; we built forts and climbed trees. We skinny-dipped in every creek, tank and horse trough we could find. We ate ripe and raw persimmons, peanuts, pecans and the kernels out of stinging nettles. The last, even though we told each other that eating them would drive one crazy. The sand dunes around Carbon were ideal for fort-building, pie-melon hurling and occasionally, sand fights.

The Death of Hous

On Sunday, October 22, 1944, World War II was still a short time away from ending. Hous O'Brien still had two sons in the South Pacific. It was the day his wife Fanny became a widow when Hous died of injuries sustained in an automobile accident. A third son, just back from the Pacific in the Marine Corp duty, was driver of the car. The fourth son was still at home in Carbon with his mother. The Someday Journalist was 12 years old.

Hous and Fanny also had two daughters. The oldest, Lorena (by his first wife Ella who died during the flu epidemic of 1918), lived in Carbon with her husband H.L. (Shorty) Thompson and their two small children, Gatha and Lindon. The other daughter by Fanny lived in Abilene with her husband John. (The 12-year-old and the son back from the Marines were by Fanny. They had lost another daughter, Bobby Nell, in 1935 to pneumonia.) The two sons still in the war were by his first wife.

When his wife died, Hous, with three little ones had wooed Fanny, a Draughon's Business College student in Fort Worth. Fanny submitted and helped raise his three and their children.

The tragedy happened like this. Hous and son-in-law Shorty had jobs in Sundown (in West Texas) where a minor oil boom was underway. Lorena, the kids and Hous had come home to Carbon for the weekend and were headed back. Marine J. C. chose to ride back as far as Abilene where he was meeting a girl. He was driving the 1939 Ford and at Elmdale, just east of Abilene, where highway construction was underway, he missed or over-corrected a turn; the car turned over; Hous, without seat belts in that day, fell out.

Word came to Carbon. Neighbor Clarence Hastings (Fanny's brother) and his wife Nina and Fanny rode in the cab of his early vintage GMC pickup (he was a mail carrier and had a gas card), and their daughter Betty and the 12-year-old rode in the back. First they headed to Hendricks Hospital. "He's not here." Then to St. Ann's where they were met by injured Lorena

8

who reported, "He's gone."

Widowed, Fanny, who had never worked outside the home, now had to find work: picking trash out of peanuts on a moving belt, and also as a receptionist at a chiropractic center. The son had to go to the big school at Cisco where he was out of place. They lived in the Denslow Hotel, an old boom-time relic. She worked at Boss Manufacturing; fell on ice, broke a wrist. It didn't work out; back to Carbon. He finished high school, washing dishes at John's Cafe, cleaning up.

Aunt Nina, knowing that neither he nor his mother had extra money, bought his $32 graduation ring.

Never Again

The one horror memory of my unbridled youth was the demonstration of needle eating -- done on a school stage and often impromptu for others in my hopes to become a magician. It consisted of placing sewing needles, one after the other into one's mouth and then rolling up a little ball of thread and putting it in with the needles, and then with great fanfare, reaching in to grasp one end of the thread and pulling it out from one's mouth with the needles threaded on it. Great applause -- and great stupidity. I knew the technique and did it often, flawlessly, but would I ever do it again? Never! And I regret doing it then.

It's a wonder we reached maturity.

Magic and Me

It all began in a "dime store" in Gorman, the little town we sometimes went to from Carbon for doctors, shopping and outings. We generally went by bus. It was a little inner-city line (Texas, New Mexico and Oklahoma) run, I think by Mr. Johnny Aaron. J. C. Poe usually was the driver of this line which went

9

from Abilene to San Antonio. It was handy. We had no car.

Name of the store I don't remember but it was one of those old "all purpose" places. Some called them "racket stores." Think minor, locally owned Woolworths. On a counter I found some magic tricks for sale. The one I could afford (maybe a quarter) was a paper-folding miracle that turned a piece of paper into a dollar bill. Wow. I began entertaining (?) everybody I saw: friends, family and strangers. That set the bait.

Later in the back of a comic book, I found an ad for Douglas Magic Land, "just down the road in Dallas." I sent my dime and got a real, genuine catalog by return mail, filled with every imaginable miracle. I was truly hooked.

There were many inexpensive items and more elaborate tools too to fool people. I ordered what little I could afford, and began waiting the next day at the Carbon post office to see if my package had arrived. Meredith Black was the postal clerk, and she knew me by heart. Finally, oh finally, it came, and I was a true magician with a "box of tricks." I did shows in class, on the front porch, living rooms all over, and obviously bored people to death with my "talents."

After a number of orders I got a flyer from Douglas inviting me to the Texas Magicians Association annual convention. Wow. I had been recognized. As a poor public school student, certainly I couldn't go, but I dreamed.

Many years later, after college, after the Army, I did go to State Conventions in Dallas and San Antonio. Here I saw professionals and amateurs like me all enjoying performing and watching others perform in real live magic shows. I remember Dia Vernon, Mark Wilson (before he got big), Harry Blackstone Jr. (who was then a U-T student), Willard the Wizzard, and

10

dozens more, some of whom are still active, but most gone. At each I learned new things and broadened my interest, and at dealer booths and through wonderful mail order, I acquired and acquired every conceivable trick I could afford and some I couldn't.

Later, again after adulthood I learned of the International Brotherhood of Magicians, joined and have collected their monthly magazine (The Linking Ring) since about 1957. These I have as well as boxes of props and paraphernalia for me doing "The Greatest Show (of its kind) on Earth."

Horror show: a Halloween night show at the school in Albany, which I did because a friend who had booked it got sick and asked me to fill in -- unprepared and not ready for such a rowdy crowd.

I still read but do very little or no demonstrations. I guess I pretty well gave up the foolish idea of becoming a world-famous entertainer traveling the world doing magic and writing the great American novel in my spare time. Why did I give up? I learned that groceries cost money and that I really didn't have the talent or wouldn't take the time to practice to be good. I figure my son or grandchildren will acquire my vast collection.

Early Ad Sales

Carbon, TX, High School, 1948-49--The advertisements supporting the publication of the Carbon Wolverine Annual Yearbook had been sold throughout the county because students got time out of class to travel and call on merchants to collect what amounted to donations to the school. Few ads would be seen except by students and their relatives.

But as the printer's deadline approached for final copy to be turned in, all of the collected calling cards, scraps of copy notes and student-scribbled ad instructions lay undisturbed on a desk in the school library.

Recognizing the possible trauma if something

11

wasn't done to bring some order to the mess, the Would-Be Editor, who at that time had no career plans, in fact no plans at all except making it through the day until the bell rang, took it upon himself to take the mess home. With a ballpoint pen (then relatively new; Sharpies and their ink had not even been thought of), the fledgling editor began to calculate the size of the purchase, draw appropriate borders to fit, and ink in "sparkling" ad copy, not forgetting to put in the advertiser's name, location and phone number. The end result: crude by any measure, but in time to make the print deadline. He garnered much teacher approval for his responsible act, if not for his talent at lettering.

Trick or Trick

Diversions were limited but not without hilarity; Halloween night was big, long before the highly organized innocent trick or treating and commercialism known today. Ours consisted of turning over outhouses, especially the one at Merrit Dunn's house. Because Merrit was the local editor of a little four-page newspaper, I always felt a bit of guilt in participating in the upending of his (un-)sanitary facility. Actually he was pretty much the local fall guy -- small in stature and tight as Dick's hat band probably because he had to be, considering the income he had from the limited number of advertisers in that small town. He smoked cheap Bugler tobacco, which he rolled into passable cigarettes. He was jokingly referred to as "Wolf Eggs" Dunn because he had once fallen for a jesting gag that So and So had discovered a wolf's nest on the edge of town. Poor Merrit: he and his wife hand set (letter by letter) the type for limited news, and the rest was mostly boilerplate by a company that swapped newsprint in exchange for their patent medicine advertising printed thereon. I'm glad to say that many years later when we bought his paper for $10 and good will, we engineered a silver platter and salute to him and his wife for their many years of diligent news labors.

After dealing with Merrit's outhouse and others, the gang would go "tic-tacking," which consisted of attaching a waxed string to the window screen of assorted villagers and then rubbing the string with a bit of resin, which made a horribly scary (to us) sound that highly disturbed the occupants. I don't think we ever asked for treats.

One of our clever associates came up with the idea of having one of us stand on either side of State Highway 6, holding out our hands as though we were stretching a wire or string across the highway, much to the dismay of drivers of the few autos that passed that way, especially at night. We also took watermelons from loaded trucks slowed on the steep hill east of town on the Gorman highway. And hitchhiking once to the 10¢ King Theater movie in Gorman got into a Cadillac driven by a drunk ex-serviceman just back from the South Pacific, who didn't plan to ever sober up. We were more careful of rides later.

The Jokes

What's black and white and red all over? It used to be a newspaper, but now the kids say: A blushing zebra.

* * *

I used to be an old newspaper man; then I found out there wasn't any money in old newspapers.

* * *

Some newspapers are black and white, but the (local paper) is always read.

* * *

I've seen some funny things in the newspapers--besides fish and chips.

13

CHAPTER 2
Basic Training

FT. BLISS, TX, MARCH, 1954 -- After an all-night bus ride from Abilene, the half dozen inductees arrived at their new home at El Paso. Quickly routed to a mess hall for breakfast, most ate little on weak stomachs.

They'd been sworn in by a draft board official in Abilene, given their military identification numbers and told to memorize them on the way west, so they were officially in the United States Army.

He's Officially US54147000

At Abilene, the inductor accompanied the men to the bus station to make sure that none walked away. He gave one of the troops the papers for all the men and warned him not to lose them. As they climbed on the Greyhound, he told them, "First stop, Ft. Bliss, next stop, Korea; have fun."

The sun bore down and the wind blew as the little group joined a much larger group of inductees to be housed in temporary quarters before being assigned to a training unit for eight weeks of hell. All thought that the "permanent" housing would be better than the temp which dated from the horse calvary days of WWII.

"No Juarez"

After repeated warnings of court martial, all were advised not to even think about leaving quarters until told to move.

Sure enough, a number of the younger draftees couldn't resist and made their way off post and across the bridge to Juarez where they were intercepted by M.P.s, which resulted in suffering for others, who were denied even going to the 3.2 beer hall PX because of the infractions.

After the truants returned, it was the first time that most had witnessed rear-end scrubbing with G.I. brushes of the now-suffering offenders. It was not

14

pretty.

The permanent housing did not prove superior: it was four men to a shack that had been used to house German prisoners of war after the Big One. Two stacked cots, foot lockers, a butt can and a latrine 50 yards down the way. Intensive training began the day after moving in.

The introduction from the drill sergeant, a veteran back from bloody Korea, was anything but pleasant. First off: "I hope you people have given your hearts to God, because from this day forward, your ass belongs to me." He meant it.

Double Shots

We were among many who were administered two sets of shots. The first round was bad enough, but then word came later that we had to re-submit; the shot clinic had lost (?) all the records, so line up and take it all again, in both arms.

The desert fresh air, exercise and maybe allergies resulted in lots of extra nasal and throat volume which generally needed regular disposal for most of the troops. Drill instructors continually repeated: "You might not want to be planting those oysters just anywhere because you may be lying down on them soon."

The first weeks were hell, but as time went along, even the frailest of us toughened up, and the bounty of food at every meal was devoured with relish. Result: improved health and maybe attitude. There even came a time when we began considering ourselves soldiers.

Tie a towel to your bunk if you're on K.P. to be awakened EARLY. Last ones in the mess hall, go to pots and pans. And don't leave valuables anywhere: one G.I. hung his fatigue jacket on a hook, forgetting

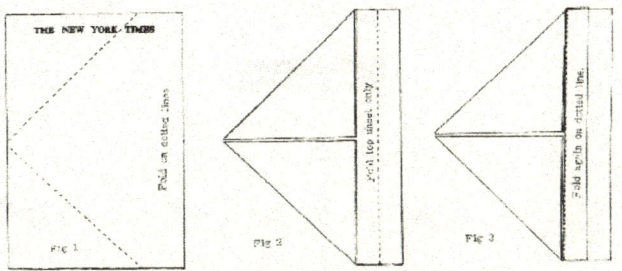

Pressman's Hat

How to make a Pressman's hat -- be the envy of your neighorbhood. Much research has been done to establish the origin of this unique headpiece. It has never been determined when or where the first paper hat was worn, but records show that it was being worn in the United States as early as 1748. The handmade hat is worn by pressmen as protection against ink, grease, oil and paper lint which might otherwise get in their hair. Start with a full double sheet of newspaper in the position as shown in figure 1 on next page. The heading "New York Times" shows the position of the paper.

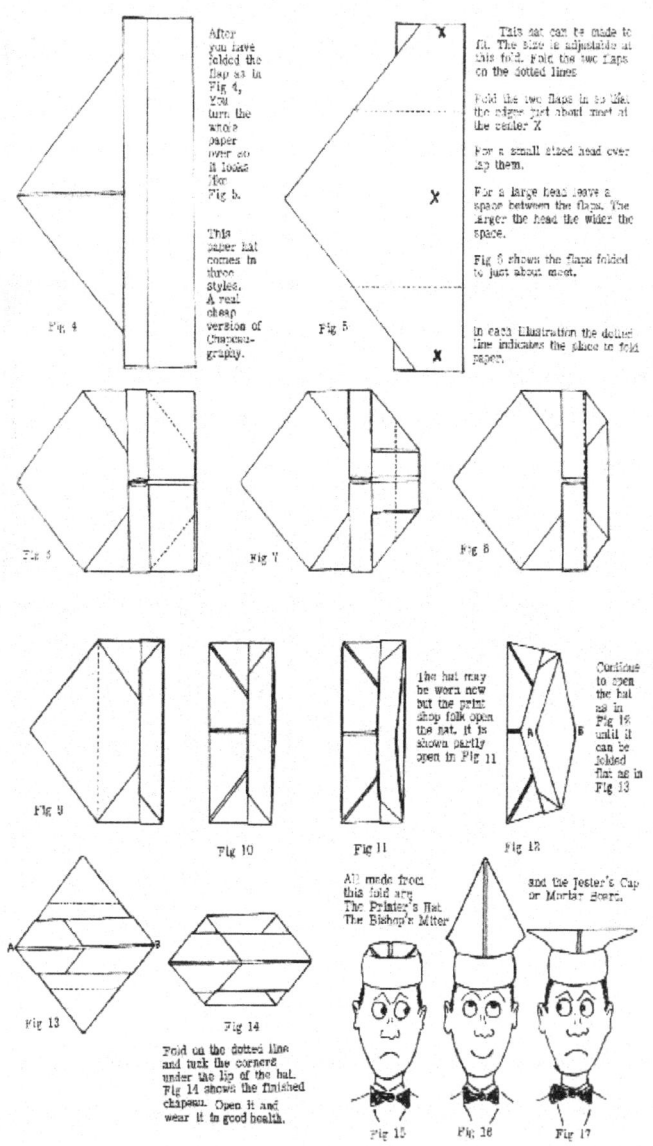

After you have folded the flap as in Fig 4, you turn the whole paper over so it looks like Fig 5.

This paper hat comes in three styles. A real cheap version of Chapeaugraphy.

Fig. 4

This hat can be made to fit. The size is adjustable at this fold. Fold the two flaps on the dotted lines

Fold the two flaps in so that the edges just about meet at the center X

For a small sized head over lap them.

For a large head leave a space between the flaps. The larger the head the wider the space.

Fig 6 shows the flaps folded to just about meet.

In each illustration the dotted line indicates the place to fold paper.

Fig 5

Fig 6   Fig 7   Fig 8

The hat may be worn now but the print shop folk open the hat. It is shown partly open in Fig 11

Continue to open the hat as in Fig 12 until it can be folded flat as in Fig 13

Fig 9   Fig 10   Fig 11   Fig 12

All made from this fold are The Printer's Hat The Bishop's Miter

and the Jester's Cap or Mortar Board.

Fig 13   Fig 14

Fold on the dotted line and tuck the corners under the lip of the hat. Fig 14 shows the finished chapeau. Open it and wear it in good health.

Fig 15   Fig 16   Fig 17

17

that his billfold was in it. Result: report and start long tedious process of rescuing i.d.s and other valuable documents. Cash? It probably wasn't much.

To a person, the draftees, if asked today would say in unison: "I wouldn't take for the experience but I don't want any more." They claim the volunteer Army is better today. The volunteers then had R.A. prefixes to their I.D. number. Inductees had U.S. I.D.s.

G.I. Humor

Way before daylight, Sgt. Brown had the entire Battery out on the parade ground for calisthenics. He led and expected the troops to follow even though most could not see each other much less him at that early hour. As exercises continued, a voice from one corner came loud and clear, "What color is shit?" In reply: "Brown." And then, "What kind of brown?" And from another undetectable area, "Sgt. Brown."

Funny, but painful, again. The sarge ran us all around the parade field three times before dismissing.

Many days later at the 3.2 beer hall, when he was attempting to prove that he was human too, he wept as he told his tablemates that he had once had a promising career in radio but could never go back because he had ruined his voice screaming at greenhorns trying to make soldiers out of them. The cycle was eight weeks, and he'd get a new batch of boots.

The weather was foul; the sand ground into every opening and pore. The overnight "in the field" was miserable for all, sleeping in pup tents, on G.I. blankets which didn't soften the prairie gravel.

Professional Goof-Off

And then the 50-mile hike loomed. Even short jaunts were hell, especially for those of us on the end in "rout march" (out of step) who had to sweat blood to keep up. Many didn't and fell by the wayside. There was one, whose identity will remain anonymous because the statute of limitations may not have run out, who felt certain that he could not make that big march. He devised a plan.

He realized that the officer of the day and others each morning inspected the cabins to make sure there were no stragglers and that the night-soaked mattresses (actually thin pads) had all been rolled up for better drying. The recruit secured allergy drops and cough medicine bottles and borrowed other medical containers and bottles from friends and neighbors. He carefully laid them alongside his cot, crawled into the covers and went fast to sleep, getting the first rest he'd had in weeks. Sometime later the inspectors did come by. They looked -- and passed on.

The unit was a mix of youngsters and some not-so-young. The Journalism grad was among the older. One guy was a science major hooked on spiders. The early weeks were killers. Many had gone to school days and worked nights for years, and to put it mildly, we were soft. But you know in about the sixth or seventh week, the exercise, solid meals and self-discipline of regular hours began to be reflected in better health and attitude. That is not to say that we were all trained military killing machines, but at least we were becoming soldiers. And even the rag-knots were beginning to take shape.

19

Korea or Georgia

And the final weekday came. The top Sarge called the troops together to read assignments. Almost in a sing-song, the words came: Anderson, Brown, Crystal, FECOM, Dixon, FECOM, Martin, FECOM, FECOM, and FECOM and FECOM -- and without being told, we all knew, it meant Far East Command -- Korea.

On and on it droned, until finally, the journalist heard "O'Brien" -- "Cryptography." He blinked. His eyes glazed and his mind asked "What's that?" He then realized that his background of keyboarding with good eye-hand coordination meant something after all.

He was told to report to the orderly room for travel arrangements, where he picked up airline tickets from El Paso to Atlanta, Georgia, with a hold-over in Amon Carter Field (before DFW) between Dallas and Fort Worth and to report to Fort Gordon, Georgia after the leave. It was a five-hour DC4 flight to Amon Carter and a five-hour Greyhound bus ride back west to Abilene.

20

CHAPTER 3
The Basement Beacons

It probably started in Carbon High School in the late '40s. For some unknown reason, it developed that I had an exceptional knack for typing. Teacher J. W. Turner recognized this, and knowing that with my family and financial status, opportunities for college were slim, he recommended to a community college friend that if he'd find me a job, it could mean a college education.

And so I wound up as a part-time "printer's devil" at the Cisco newspaper office, sweeping out and counting out papers to carrier boys evenings and early Sunday mornings.

Impressed that I was trying to work my way through college, as he had done, the publisher/editor recognized that I needed to learn a trade that would further help sustain my education. He sat me down one day at the complicated Linotype machine and convinced me that I could learn the 100-plus keys on the keyboard.

Eventually I did. The machine, now obsolete, was a mechanical marvel then that assembled individual letters, spaces, punctuation marks and space bands into a line and then exposed the lot to molten lead, resulting in a kicked out "line of type" -- IF the operator had all settings properly adjusted and did everything in proper sequence. If all was done correctly, repeatedly, one line of ready-to-print news type and/or headlines and/or lines to go into an advertisement would be assembled in a catch tray. To say that operating the machine was complicated is a colossal understatement. But it's part of the tale.

After the community college, I was able to move on to a senior university, and with my type-setting skills found employment with the daily newspaper.

Korea Looms

The dark cloud at that time was the fact that the Korean War was raging and men were being drafted right and left and sent directly to the battlefield. My age and health made me a prime prospect for a uniform, but I was striving to finish my degree before being called up. Thanks to an understanding Eastland County draft board secretary, my name was shuffled back after each of my regular "just one more semester" pleas.

But eventually my "Congratulations, you have been selected to serve, etc." letter arrived almost coinciding with my diploma, and within weeks, I was on my way to eight weeks of basic training, as US Pvt. O'Brien. Well, after four years of working nights and going to class days, all the hikes, drills and training of basic came close to taking me out permanently. Just about the time I began to feel better and "be trained," it was all over.

Cryptography?

And then God showed me once again that He was in charge and was preparing me for what lay ahead.

On the day of assignment announcements, all were justifiably nervous. Man after man heard Infantry, "FECOM" (Far East Command--Korea), and we all sweated blood. And after tension reached the boiling point, finally, "O'Brien, Cryptography School, Camp

Gordon, GA."

Whew! Not only did I not know how to spell it, I didn't even know what it was." In due time I learned that it had to do with coding, and I finally recognized that some dear assignment sergeant and/ or civilian had seen the bulk of my military records of shots, skills, temperament and that I had not heisted hubcaps, maybe, and recognized that I might be a likely candidate to operate machinery necessary to do code work. Praise be that person(s) who picked me for that.

After four weeks of non-classified Cryptography school, we went into a "holding pattern" of routine Army-famous chores -- K.P. duty in the kitchens and the parking lots, barracks, and parade grounds policing, until our security clearances came through proving that we were in fact, trustworthy, loyal, courteous and kind.

And when I was found pure, I went into the fenced area for the classified part of the training. And would you believe that my hand-eye, typing coordination stood me in good stead here. I was named outstanding of the class.

Shortly after we went into Augusta's Boom-Boom Club for temperate celebrating, some of us were called in for a special interview. "What now, pray tell? Did the Boom-Boom Club sink our wholesomeness?" Alas, no, we were being checked to see if we were qualified for a special top-secret assignment.

Private Compartments

Two others and I were picked to board a train (private roomettes?) bound for Washington, D.C. where we were being assigned to WHASA (White House Army Signal Agency) with headquarters in an abandoned auto garage, but duty in the basement of THE House where President and Mrs. Eisenhower dwelled, providing top secret communications between him and all his various agency lieutenants -- State, Treasurer, Defense, etc., etc., etc. And wouldn't you know it, the machinery we used wasn't terribly different to all the machines we'd been exposed to. Coincidence? Guidance? Take your choice. I choose guidance.

Singles in D.C.

We lived in apartments and wore civilian clothes in the Washington of the early '50s--street cars and an exciting downtown, plus all the museums, galleries, monuments, embassies, nearby historical sites and all the other "bright lights" you could imagine for a young WASP raised in the farming area in the middle of Texas. We worked shifts--eight on, sixteen off--so there was plenty of time for major exploration. An exciting time.

The work? Stressful to say the least, but filled with pride. We were dealing constantly with officials around the world, and the very art of coding required intense concentration. Most of us were drafted G.I.s, and we were working for and with career officers who demanded perfection -- to save their heads. As for the crews, it was walking a straight line -- to foul up was automatic transfer to a line outfit where one soldiered.

One in particular, I remember, was caught shoplifting at Hecht's Dept. Store. He was gone before sundown.

Movies with Ike

Fringe benefits? Sitting on the back row when the President and Mrs. Eisenhower and their guests watched movies during the evening shift. (He preferred westerns, she musicals). On the midnight shift we took turns either sleeping in the recliners in Sherman Adams's emergency office, one of many of the emergency underground shelters provided for the first family and close staff. Some nights we utilized the emergency cots and linen stored there for a really good night's sleep. We were often disturbed by being called to handle important communications. (We slept when we could to be able to explore the city by day.)

There were House telephone operators, radio operators and maintenance personnel all pulling their Army M.O.S. duties for WHASA. All of the shifts came through a special gate on the north side. There were nights when the Secret Service had concerns about attacks, etc., and we all went on high alerts. We also took turns going out to a remote fire station where we spent the shifts standing by in case there was a fire in the House. The House telephone switchboard number then was Sterling 30333.

Red Phone Duty

One of our most important duties was helping test the famous Red Phone which was being developed at that time in the '50s. You'll remember it was an ingenious system to connect the U.S.A.'s top nerve center with the Soviet Union's Kremlin headquarters. Each morning when we were on the midnight shift, one of us would go at 6 a.m. to the Oval Office, pick up the Red Phone and make coded contact with a counterpart on the other end of the line, assigned to the American Embassy in Moscow who had gone into the Soviet nerve center to talk with us.

High drama? When President Eisenhower had a heart attack in Denver, it was Crisis time for all hands.

In all, a short tour: arrived D.C. in October as a private, 1954; to discharge on the two-year service, March 1956, as a Staff Sergeant. Much inducement and encouragement were offered to stay for a four-year sign-up, with promises for continued promotions.

Family obligations back in West Texas prompted a "Thank you, but no thanks."

And so back to the newspaper business where I've been ever since.

Len Hickman

I met Len Hickman, a totally collegiant frat type from Port Norris, N.J., when the group was taken from Fort Gordon to the train station in Augusta, Georgia, to go to D.C. Also picked to go was Andy McCollum of Oklahoma City, who had lived off-base with his wife Barbara. The fourth man picked to go was Bill Sermons from Nags Head, N.C. So there were four of us (plus a wife) put into private roomettes for the overnight ride north.

In D.C. we reported to W.H.A.S.A. headquarters (an out-of-the- way former auto repair center near Rock Creek Park), where we were told to find places to live and report back tomorrow. We were told of a rental facility near 14th St., for temporary "bunking,"

26

and that's what it was -- college-dormitory style. It wasn't very desirable so we looked for something else. I don't remember where the McCollums landed.

We found an apartment in a highrise near 14th St. which Hickman, Sermons and I shared for some time. There was a miniature kitchen, a bedroom with two singles, and we alternated on the couch in the so-called living room. After we started working shifts, we even had our NCO Sgt. Russell come in one night for supper with us, spaghetti as I remember. A shift Chief named Arnot, now deceased, was native of nearby Breckenridge north of Eastland.

Hickman and Sermons had some sort of falling out, and Sermons moved out.

Hickman found us a basement apartment below a dentist's office, just off DuPont Circle in a '50s "collegiate" style neighborhood. We needed a third to afford it, so we recruited Jim Hartzell from Detroit who was already in the outfit and fortunately at the time needing a new place to live. The three of us were well looked after by the receptionist upstairs. In fact, Andy and Barbara joined us later again, in an apartment on an upper floor of the rowhouse. We all often sat on the front stoop, visiting and watching the then interesting safe neighborhood. Peoples Drug Store with a lunch counter was nearby.

As time moved along, Barbara announced that they were expecting their first baby, which they had already named "Boo" -- as in boo-boo. We looked after her on shifts that Andy had to work apart from ours.

Here too, Len bought an antique auto, acquired Keystone auto insurance (which soon cancelled him due to excessive breakdowns) and suddenly we had transport beyond the fascinating trolly system. We even went to the Gettysburg Battle site. Len asked me to join him on a long weekend to his home in New Jersey. I met his folks; his dad ran an oyster house and claimed that Delaware Bay oysters were better than Chesapeake.

Suspicions grew when Len, after a look at the Atlantic City boardwalk and pier, etc., took me to an unusal bar. Especially for a mid-Texan, I saw things that I didn't understand. Men in drag! Dressed as women. The waiters and entertainers, were most unusual. Later at a dinner with his family, his sister asked, "You didn't take him to that horrible bar, did you?" I kept quiet to his response. There was no 'Don't ask, don't tell' policy at that time.

The upside is that Len never made any sort of untoward overtures; we were just fellow soldiers who had been drafted, found ourselves in a choice assignment, and were friends and apartment mates. But I did witness his acquaintances in the area, so Jim Hartzell and I spent a lot of time visiting all the attractions of D.C. Jim was in love with Joan of Massachusetts, one of the employees in then Sen. John Kennedy's office, who later married. Jim's 2-year enlistment ended first and he left. Mine came up before Len's.

When he got out, Len stayed in D.C. and became a hotel/motel executive director in the city; he was an extraordinary social and party person so we know he did well. I have since learned through others that his health failed (suspicion prevails) and is probably dead by now. I've talked to Jim a few times; he's the retired J. Walter Thompson employee who coined the famous Chevrolet slogan -- HOT DOGS, BASEBALL AND CHEVROLET. He lives in Detroit.

28

Coming Home

Re-upping was very much on the minds of the U.S. two-year draftee in March of 1956 stationed at the White House. The R.A.s (Regular Army enlistees) had more time to serve.

It was pretty much pre-determined that the Would-Be Journalist would muster out. For two reasons: one a widowed mother back at home he felt responsibility for, and the fact of the unknown big question mark looming over the heads of all serving in that highly critical assignment.

The WHASA had a record of never having had a court martial -- for a simple reason: if one goofed or fouled up, that person would be immediately transferred to another unit and court martialed. There were several we saw go wrong with the law and find themselves stripped of security clearance, White House pass, and doing duty at Fort Meyers or further afield.

The three who had been apartment mates, all drafted college graduates, went separate ways. The Journalist invited his mother to fly to D.C. for her look at the nation's capital and all its treasures that he had been exploring and enjoying for two rather leisurely years. As a further treat, they returned together to West Texas by train by way of Chicago, St. Louis, Dallas, and on to Abilene. He quickly readjusted to civilian life and returned to the night shift at the Abilene Reporter-News, once again as a Linotype operator.

The pay was good and the hours were not bad after he learned to go home and go to bed after getting off work at midnight or later. This offered free daylight hours to accomplish things rather than going out with other employees after work for late-night heavy meals and gallons of coffee, which wrecked the rest of the night and most of the next day when one had to be back at work at 3 p.m.

The machine operation wasn't as challenging as it once was, but it did keep him in the proximity of where he eventually wanted to be -- the editorial department.

He eventually worked himself up to a daytime shift, which gave him the opportunity to work after hours for neighboring weekly newspapers, which were continually needing part-time helpers. At one, he did serious editing after the publisher was killed in an auto accident. There he not only read and developed the incoming copy, generating some himself, but also set it on the Linotype machine, put it together, and printed it on the antique press. He even handled advertising that came in, so all-in-all he was furthering his skills in many areas for publishing. It was all education.

Jerry Strader

His name was Jerry Strader and he came to the Reporter-News in about 1956, and it was quickly obvious that he was a hand-picked protege of the Harte-Hanks newspaper chain. He had been told to work in every department, and we all were told to teach him everything we knew about our various departments.

One could tell that he was above average and obviously bound for great things with the giant media corporation. Even so, he was also a young, newly married young man of some 20 years. We knew he came from Greenville and had attracted the eye of some executive at the headquarters, which was then in Corpus Christi.

Still, he was a nice guy and a friend to all. I was just back from the Army, lived on Victoria Street, and after we had become friends, invited him and his wife Julie and him over one evening to listen to records on my new hi-fi stereo. They brought their baby -- a small dachshund, as I remember, in a V.W.

I had a new Fred Waring album that I really enjoyed and wanted to share with them. Waring and his Pennsylvanians had been in Abilene for a concert at Hardin-Simmons, and it had been the first time I had heard their version of the "Battle Hymn of the Republic", which is now a standard classic.

They were equally thrilled with the entire album, and when we reached the crescendo of the Battle Hymn, we turned that early-day stereo sky high for a most dramatic musical experience.

The last time I talked to Jerry he had just taken a top position with a Chicago newspaper chain. He and Julie were still together. He had made it to the top; wonder where he is today?

CHAPTER 4
A Partner

Then in August of 1959, I found my true lifetime partner. A college student who worked nights as a long distance telephone operator, back when there were such things, and she sang in the church choir where I attended. It was learned later that my sister and some of her girlfriends pretty much helped bring it about.

She was told to look for the blonde-headed young man who always had an uncombed "rooster-tail" on the back of his head. He was told to look at that pretty auburn-haired girl always in the frilly dress in the choir. He did and she did, and after church on a Sunday night, he asked and she accepted a Coke date. They agreed to meet again. It developed that she lived with her mother and brother not far from where he lived. He called. She responded to an invitation for a dinner date. It was to a well-known fish restaurant where they became better acquainted. Meals, movies and parking talks became paramount for both, and in time they made plans, setting a tentative date for sometime "next year." The date turned out to be June 18, 1960, at Calvary Baptist Church in Abilene. It was a nice but less than elaborate wedding because neither were rolling in extra cash.

Joining forces in a FHA frame house on an expansion street, they began their good life together.

The Honeymoon

After the wedding, we drove to Merkel of all places for a quiet meal together at the truck stop. The son of the deceased publisher for whom I had worked part-time was there and treated us to our post-wedding

32

supper.

True to tradition, Gaynell and I did not see each other the day prior to the wedding on June 17, so I have no idea how she spent that day but I well remember how my day was spent.

As best as I knew how then, the house was tidied. Surely the trash was taken out. Surely new linen was found and put on. It was a little two-bedroom, one-bath, little den-office-3rd bedroom-FHA-Veteran frame at 893 N. LaSalle St. in northwest Abilene, just off N. 10th and Pioneer Dr. I had financed it and had lived there for maybe a little over a year.

The wedding site was to be at the church "just down the street" at 12th St. and Minter Lane. Gaynell lived on North 10th.

On the fateful wedding day, there were many chores to be done. Guess which ones got done? For one thing, I drove all over Abilene looking for a drugstore where I wasn't known. Remember the '60s were the days when certain things were not openly displayed but kept "under the counter," to be asked for at the pharmacy. Finally, on the far south side, my mission was accomplished.

I'm pretty sure I also got a haircut in the neighborhood, and you could bet I didn't let it be known what I was preparing for because I didn't want to be teased about what was coming. I'll bet I also washed the 1960 Nash Rambler Station Wagon I had traded a slick 1957 Chevrolet Bel Air four-door for not so long before.

Surely my payroll and vacation checks had been cashed. If there was a checking account, I don't remember it, and there were no credit cards for us in those days. I know I was ill-prepared financially.

But

The one chore I should have done did not get done.

When the bride and groom arose the morning after the wedding, there was no coffee, milk, bread, or cereal in the house.

Obviously the thought of breakfast had not crossed my mind.

Sunday morning we awoke to discover that I had made bad plans. So we pretty much went without. After packing, we bounded for the Texas Coast.

Hungry, still excited and wide-eyed, we made it on State 36 as far as Coleman, where we found a downtown Sunday dinner cafe.

Next stop was Austin, where we found an inexpensive motel on the main highway. We even went to church that Sunday night, and I think were introduced as newlyweds. And then to San Antonio, where I think we stayed on Broadway because I remember we ate at Earl's.

Remember, I had not been driving all that long and certainly not in big towns.

The fact is I learned to drive AFTER I came home from the Army, and finally bought my first car, a '53 or '54 Chevrolet coupe (later the '57 Chevy Belair). We weren't deprived. Just forced by circumstances to walk, take the bus, or stay in one place.

We made it to Corpus Christi and the Ebb Tide Motel on North Beach. We sunned on the sand at the beach maybe ventured into Corpus proper, and maybe eventually got all the way to Padre Island. Anyway we sunburned, but it was a marvelous learning time together. Details elude but the thrill experience has never gone away. We've been many places since and done many wonderful things, but there has never been anything like that special first time together.

She sacrificed her college plans to work days as church secretary and he continued to work days at the

Reporter days and nights at the weeklies.

Both had humble but honest backgrounds, from an assortment of bloodlines. His great-grandfather came from Cork, probably either as a deck hand or stow-away, and got off the boat in Mobile, Alabama. Probably Catholic, it came to pass that he met a Baptist girl in Arkansas, which started the lineage.

Gaynell's folks came from English and German backgrounds and out of East Texas, yet wound up in West Texas.

He was the youngest of seven and she was the oldest of five.

His mother once questioned the advisability of his "going into Journalism" because she had visions of drunks and dopeheaded poets.

Gaynell grew up, finished school in Rotan, Texas, and went to Midland to work for Southwestern Bell, with plans for college later. One of her two sisters had already married and moved to California, leaving a sister and two brothers with their mother, who was soon to divorce their dad. The older brother finished school there and started HSU; the two younger ones moved to Abilene with their mother, and the girl graduated and soon joined her sister in California.

During that first year of marriage, as is true with most new unions, things were pretty tough at times, money-wise. The Would-Be Editor was working days at the Reporter and evenings at the neighboring country papers. Gaynell had become secretary of their church in order to work days instead of the night telephone company job. We always regretted that she was not able to finish college.

At her encouragement and suggestions, the new husband was admonished to keep trying for moving into the editorial department which came about -- at a salary drop. And it was back to nights for him. As an ambulance chaser and hospital patient and obituary recorder, it was journalism in the raw: much better training than the years of textbook exposure. This was during heady times when a dozen Atlas missile sites and as many Nike missile sites were being built around Abilene in response to protection for the Dyess AFB bomber base during that Cold War era.

A Cub Gets Going

One day as he was recovering from a bout of flu, Reporter Editor Ed Wishcamper, remembering that the would-be journalist had inquired about moving into the editorial department, called and asked if he was game for an assignment.

The answer was yes, and he headed north in a 1958 staff car to Stamford to cover a real live story. A delegation from Washington and elsewhere was surveying certain areas to determine if a new saline-removal system might be usable in some of the less than ideal waterways of West Texas. He asked questions, made volumes of notes, and called in at 12 noon as warned in advance, to make the afternoon edition. Then he speeded back south through Abilene on U.S. 277, headed for Winters where the same group had flown to look at another possible test site, and repeated his questions and note-taking.

Hurrying back after dark, he went to the paper, found a desk and wrote many pages; this was back when papers used paste pots, putting them in long strings. In his case, probably three or four pages. A wise and skilled Night Desk Editor Jack Holden whittled it down to a manageable, meaningful one-page message that made the morning front page with his byline right up there under the three-column headline. Memory is that nothing ever came of the saline-test visit.

The legendary West Texas Editor Frank Grimes was in charge of the Editorial Department and apparently

36

saw hope in the "New Cub." It could have been partly as the result of our having visited him along with the beloved black janitor, Earl, at the T.B. Hospital where the old man was failing.

Super Editor Frank Grimes

It has always been a treasured memory that I had the honor of working, if not with, at least, technically under and at the same time as the fabled Super Editor Frank Grimes of the Harte-Hanks Group. He was a tall, lanky, true humanitarian, weaver of just the right words, and he didn't waste a one in print. I remember that he was especially kind to those of us new to the newsroom who aspired to be journalists. He knew that it was an important career field.

He is best known in Central-West Texas for his lines about determining when spring actually has arrived -- not until the mesquite trees have budded out. The mesquite is a West Texas plague tree, but for oldtimers, it is the true determiner of when we've had our last freeze of winter. The paper still prints the piece when space and time permits.

My personal favorite of a Mr. Grimes pieces of prose was a brief editorial he did on safe driving. He especially bore down on drivers who dangled an arm and hand outside a car window. This was before the days of auto air conditioning.

His sage advice: always keep your hands at 10 a.m. and 2 p.m. on the steering wheel. I still try to practice that.

It was my honor to be chosen as the one to accompany Earl, the company's favorite maintenance man to Sanitarium, Texas (South of San Angelo), where Mr. Grimes lived in his final days. He knew us both and thanked us profusely for making the long trip to visit him. He loved that newspaper and its people; and everyone who read him or knew him, loved him.

The publisher then was Howard McMahon, who from his office carefully dolled out the then-new "Double-Sided" tape to the composing room to paste down metal engravings.

Mr. Mc had pulled the weary old cornball during my first interview with him, saying "You say you are not afraid of work. Does that mean you could lie down beside it and go to sleep?" Ha, Ha!

I remained silent, and he hired me anyway.

Cold War Protection

Nine Atlas Missile Silo sites were being thrown together in the early '60s as a national emergency, 24/7 construction project. They included 100-foot excavations and untested launch equipment. Workmen were being crushed, falling to their death; and otherwise were being injured virtually on an hourly basis, so keeping up with the news was not an easy matter. Later I was moved to Military Editor with a little bit more money and responsibility for keeping up with all affairs at Dyess AFB. There were also Nike missiles sites under construction.

My beat entailed constant trips to the base and covering the B-47 Bombers which then were known as "flying fuel tanks," later replaced by the bigger and more powerful B-52s. My military experience came in handy, but it was constantly a learning process. The early C-130 cargo planes also came in while I was there.

In that editorial room he was exposed to the old-time glue-pot newspaper experience.

Editor

Ed Wishcamper was a gentle, encouraging soul; Desk Editor Dick Tarpley was harsh, but extremely helpful. Once at a near-deadline, my hastily composed article hit his desk about a musical event at Dyess which featured the old-time Modernaires performing what was reported to be the Glenn Miller Band. Tarpley yelled across the room: "Mr. Military, it's probably true that they were sinning together, but I think you meant singing. Watch it."

A call came from "out of the past" from where I first worked in a newspaper office, Cisco Press Publisher, J. W. Sitton asked "Would you consider editing and running one of them if I can close a deal to buy the Eastland Telegram and the Ranger Times from Onus Dick and Joe Dennis?..."Well, I've never...but, let me talk to Gaynell, and I'll get back to you A.S.A.P." That night the die was cast: nothing ventured, nothing gained. When the couple OK'ed to Mr. Sitton, all agreed that it will be O.J.T. of the highest order.

This was about the time Editor and Mrs. were establishing themselves in Eastland; her mother and younger brother joined them there, where he finished school and joined the Marines.

A single Cisco Press printer who had worked with the Editor was a frequent visitor for meals and visits. It evolved that he began looking upstairs where Gaynell's mother lived and as things happen, they found each other for the rest of their lives.

In time, both their mothers and the Printer died and are buried at Pleasant Hill, a rural resting place, and her dad died and is buried in Pampa, beside his second wife.

And so as the world spins, and lives intertwine, they are all the product of what went before.

In January Gaynell, our six-month-old son, Vance, and the editor went to Austin. We stayed at the Driskill Hotel, had dinner at the Headliners Club, charged to Ted Read, (Sitton's partner), and an Austin lobbyist. On a given morning we went to the Capitol, and State Attorney General Waggoner Carr presented us the Bar Award and a check for $250.00 -- wow, two and a half week's worth of salary.

And cases started moving in the 91st District Court in 1964. Earl and the editor were friends until his death, as we were with his widow.

Good Friends Are Very Important

Making friends and doing small and large favors can pay off well. In the case of the Texas Good Law Enforcement Award, a friend helped make it happen.

Bill Wright of Cisco was one of the leading trial lawyers in the county in the 60's and a virtual fixture at the courthouse. Well liked, friendly and jovial to all, he was known as an "all-right guy." He gave the newspaper a lot of legal business by placing probate, estate sale, collection and other required legal notices in the paper which earned maybe five or ten cents a word each time the legal ran. It's certain that these costs were passed along to clients as legal expenses. Because he was a good news source and nice anyway, we always went out of our way to get his legals published correctly and his statements and the notarized affidavits of publication back to his office as quickly as we could. He was in our office regularly.

In early 1963, he casually remarked to the editor that

someone should check the district court criminal case filings. "You might be surprised at what you find," he said, suggesting we scan back a few months.

Next trip to the courthouse, we took a look at the filings book in the district clerk's office. Roy Lane, the clerk, also a friend and news source, helped us find and scan the books. It didn't take long to determine that there had been many cases filed, but very few moved forward. Some had been on the books for months, and not just a few, for years.

Even to the less than seasoned editor, it was obvious that the court wasn't processing the cases. The presiding judge was Turner Collie, aging and nearing retirement.

The district attorney was Earl Conner Jr., son of a prominent county family, whose dad had been a highly respected attorney before him.

Earl and his wife Edna lived next door to us on Seaman Street.

What to do? Start recording volumes of statistical data: not an easy thing what with all the other responsibilities.

Every time Attorney Wright was in, he'd ask how the research was going and suggest tips in making it all understandable to the average reader.

Publisher Sitton and the attorney, in the interest of good law enforcement insisted that I enter them in the State Bar Association's contest.

In our third year in editing, the day-to-day work went on. Our work began and the town marked the day with the 8 a.m. and 5 p.m. toots of the steam whistle provided by the James Wright family at the Modern Dry Cleaners around the corner. (James later became the

41

highly efficient chamber of commerce manager and a close friend. His son, Jim, whom we saw grow up, later was district judge and now retired chief justice of the 11th Court of Appeals in Eastland.)

It proved to be an eventful year: our first child, a son, was born in early August, so our life became even busier.

Sometime later in the fall, the editor was notified by letter that his articles had been selected for the top award, with details for an appearance and presentation at the State Bar's annual meeting in Austin in late November. Wow!

The assassination of President Kennedy changed many plans for everybody, including the Bar's get-together. We were told to await further information on the award.

CHAPTER 5
Early Editing at the Telegram

We actually worked first for Onus Dick and Joe Dennis for two months while Sitton closed the deal to buy Eastland and Ranger papers.

The Telegram became my domain, fortunately.

Sitton had suggested that I talk to Dick and Dennis because Eastland needed an editor "right now," and if we could make a deal, then the Would-Be could be busy getting his feet wet in running a small-town newspaper on his own.

Dick gave the couple a tour of the town in his pink Cadillac convertible. That and the fact that Would-Be grew up only 10 miles south in Carbon, a bedroom city to Eastland, help cast the die, and he was hired. And then came the search for housing.

After looking at a number of rentals, FHAs, etc., we pondered the purchase of a really old two-story on one of the town's best streets. A widow who lived next door had turned it into a three-unit apartment complex. It had been her deceased husband's original home, but after his first wife died, he remarried. He bought the house next door, where she now lived following his death, and she wanted to sell rather than continue in the rental business. She quoted $10,000.00 which the young couple did not have, but they pondered. It was roomy, if nothing else; no central heat or air, and showing its age. "But it has possibilities," said Gaynell, who as every women does, could envision a better day. There was not a blade of grass in the yard. There was a single driveway to the back, where there was a rented apartment over a two-car garage (known by some as a carriage house.) The main house had a rented apartment upstairs, and the bottom floor was at that time, unoccupied. And they continued to ponder as they drove back to Abilene.

This Old House

After much soul searching, they decided to buy "if she would agree to carry the note and include all of the furniture (some old and decrepit and some of antique quality). She did, and they agreed on the phone, and then we began to wonder where we would get a down payment. A listing of their visible, limited assets and a round of the commercial loan companies turned up enough to qualify as a reasonable down payment. A truck was hired to haul the few heavy possessions. They further loaded clothes and boxes, in their relatively new 1960 Nash Rambler station wagon and headed east to Eastland and S. Seaman St. to make a home.

The Labor Day weekend was spent unpacking, and he also covered his first golf tournament at Lone Cedar Country Club. On Monday he went into the holiday closed office to put out his limited tools and to get a feel of his new work space.

Tuesday would come and he would meet his associates, Publisher's wife Rex Dick, Bookkeeper Tommie June Sharp, Society Editor Carolyn Collins, Zelma Willoughby and Owner/Ad Salesman Cigar-Smoking Onus Dick, and the Sheriff cited earlier.

The 25 x 100 foot building was on the south side of the square facing the courthouse with office supplies in the front where the ladies worked and a private office for the editor and adman Dick and a vast empty back end where presses had once stood, but now used only for labeling and mailing papers and dealing with a dozen carrier boys.

Cooling was by swamp coolers and heat by Dearborn gas heaters. On nice days the rear doors and the front door were left open to take advantage of the breeze except on butchering days at the J.O. Earnest Packing Plant across the alley from the newspaper building.The squealing of dying livestock and the odor of slaughtered beef and swine was overpowering; the doors and windows often stayed closed.

And then the learning began. The Telegram was founded in 1925 and is a combination of any number of other weeklies that started and consolidated, folded or silently slipped away. Others have come and gone since. The Telegram was 188 years old in 2013.

Its sister paper, the Ranger Times, was ten miles east on what was then the old Bankhead Highway 80, now I-20. The old flatbed, two- way Duplex press, which at one time had been a printing machine for the Fort Worth Star Telegram, was there as well as Linotype machines and makeup tables.

Both papers did a lot of commercial printing (before computers and printers) in the Ranger plant, where Expert Printer Hale Dunson presided. Both papers were printed on Wednesdays with a Thursday dateline, and Saturdays with a Sunday dateline. Co-Publisher Joe Dennis presided and sold ads in Ranger, where his son Dwain was editor. Biggest advertising account in Ranger was Montgomery Ward, which had a retail store in that old 1919 oil boom town.

The new Eastland editor was an attraction,

and many popped in just to meet him and make suggestions. Bill Leslie and Dusty Rhodes introduced themselves and made it perfectly clear that they were the paper's official censors. The Editor pretended he'd never heard the word.

County School Superintendent Pop Garrett and the Lions Club enlisted the new editor and Gaynell was quickly recruited for the Civic League and Garden Club.

A town of "just" under 5,000 can have many "diversions" for the only editor in town: fires, wrecks, county and city government, and untold hundreds of public school activities, plus gossip and rumors galore.

History of the Old House

We learned that the house at 1201 S. Seaman, Eastland, Texas--what a history. Two-story classic in a grove of oak. South Seaman Street is an extension of State Highway 6 through Eastland. Six comes in on Burkett, named for an early state official and the man who developed Burkett Pecan variety, and turns on to Seaman to the Courthouse Square and on north originally. It now turns west toward Cisco.

The house was built originally with material shipped from Pennsylvania by the Prairie Oil and Gas Co. for their 1919 oil boom executives. A solid frame on pier and beams with four impressive pillars framing the front porch, it was originally the home of J. L. Clark, president of the Texas branch, and the southernmost of three in a row, all facing Seaman. Two still stands; the one in the middle has since been moved to Morton Valley, which must have been an engineering feat considering the size of the old house.

46

Bob Perkins remembers playing in the neighborhood with one of the Clark boys who climbed out a front window to sneak out of the house. The two homes remaining are of mirror image design. The twin was the Conner house, now home to a widowed Dr. Sandra Hazelip.

Well, the oil boom went bust and the oil companies moved away as they are prone to do, looking for other green pastures. The company headquarters farther down Seaman now belongs to the First Baptist Church and has been an education center, among other things.

That's the way the young married couple of one year found it in 1961. After much soul searching and "finagling," they bought it, lock, stock and barrel for $10,000.00, payable at $110.00 a month. W.D.R.'s brother, another attorney, handled the details.

Until her health began failing and she had to move to be near relatives in Comanche, Mrs. Owen was a super neighbor. We looked after her and she was good to us, probably through pity toward the young couple who came to work at the newspaper. She often called on Gaynell for assistance around her house, many times to help her button a stubborn blouse or some such. She was always quick to share cooked-too-much casseroles, etc. She was a major supporter as our children came along.

Once we with our little ones were all packed and loading the car for a trip of some sort, maybe overnight, maybe for a vacation. We had a frantic call from Mrs. Owens, "Come quick!" When we dropped all and rushed to her door, we found a commode overflowing, which she didn't know how to shut off. She was so appreciative of our help.

She often insisted that we have dinner with her and watch her slides from her many recent trips with tour groups. Sure we visited across our shared fence. Do people do that anymore?

First Months

Those first months as Editor were Master Learning Experiences. Publisher Onus handled advertising, and my job was to fill the paper with news and comments, occasionally picking up ads for him on my rounds in the company pickup. Normally our '60 Nash Rambler was left at home for Gaynell's use.

The paper's major advertisers were Safeway, A&P and Super Save (an independent) grocery. Ed Sergeant occasionally had an ad at his West Side Grocery. Texas Electric Service Co. had a quarter page every week. Lone Star Gas maybe once a month. Goodyear came to town that first year and was good for a quarter page once a week.

Mode O'Day and Altman's were the women's apparel stores, and Harelik's was a general department store. Onus worked them all. Eastland Drug (Herb Weaver and I.C. Inzer) might do some holiday ads. Tombs and Richardson rarely. Jeannette Harris ran a fabric store, and James Smith had the Men's Store. Corner Drug, Everet and Mae Plowman, didn't do much advertising, but were a popular spot.

Higginbotham and Crowell were the lumber yards of note. Victor Cornelius was a power at his V-C Menu plant, which at one time hired many employees. The

Hollywood-Vassarette Lingerie factory was going strong, and the Haydite Plant hired a fair number. T&P Railway still had a depot in Eastland and made stops and deliveries. You could get off a train but not on in Eastland.

Wendell Siebert, a native son, was school superintendent. His dad, Jess, was a barber on the west side. Willie Speaker was his shine man. Jo Jo Jones was the shine man on the north side barber shop where Tommy Clark barbered.

Interesting citizens we met during those early days were Marene Johnson-Johnson (she had had two husbands of that name) who was postmaster. She with her own funds constructed the fantastic stamp mural which still graces the P.O. lobby. She also built a flower bed on the east side with flowers appropriate to represent the American Flag. She developed Flag Day and with giant parades, programs and events, made the town very patriotic at that time. She had been a WAC and U.S.O. member.

When we hit town the Jaycees were active and were in the midst of planning the first ever annual Peanut Bowl, which was to pit the football teams of Cisco and Ranger Junior Colleges. It was to be a big day with a parade, queens, etc. Proceeds were to support the Lion's Crippled Children's Camp. Naturally, as editor, we were active in all of this and more. A later year, we horn-swaggled the 4th Army Band at Fort Hood to come here to march at halftime and perform as an effort to hold a crowd for the entire day. Our obligation was to feed the band. In a pinch we "conned" Marene and her club connections to feed the troops. They got pimento cheese sandwiches as I remember.

Clubs were big: Lions, Rotary, Jaycees, and off and on, Kiwanians. The ladies were big on clubs: Eastland Civic League and Garden Club, Music Club, the Thursday Afternoon Club which provided the library, Los Leallis and others. Eastland Memorial Hospital, the '50s homemade facility, had Candy Stripers and Volunteers at one time, later to vanish but to reappear today much stronger. The hospital was built without federal money by local craftsmen, treated by women with coffee and sweets. It's known as the hospital that doughnuts built.

Eastland Memorial Hospital

Blackwell Sanitarium in Gorman and E.L. Graham Hospital and Brown Clinic, both in Cisco, were among the early healing centers in Eastland County. Probably the first hospital was the Payne and Lovett (named for two doctors and actually cited in Ripley at one time), located just west of the present post office in Eastland.

It was local donations, fund drives and private contributions that built the E.M.H. from scratch in the 1950s, using mostly local labor and supplies in a time when medical help was otherwise scant. "New" hospitals boomed during the nationwide expansion of medical facilities, in the mid '60s and '70s, which were virtually in every town in this area. Today EMH is the only survivor, and it is thriving. EMH recently opened a badly needed, stand-alone, outpatient dialysis center which is now serving a multi-county area. And is expanding in 2019 with a Public Health Center.

A number of physicians, dentists and other

50

specialists have offices and practice in Eastland.

W.H. (Bill) Hoffmann, Jr., has been chairman of the EMH board of directors for many years and the board has led the hospital forward through good times and tough times. Along with Mr. Hoffmann, other directors include Emmett Lassater, Kael Joiner, Dr. Bob Alexander, Loretta Bulgerin, Jackie Tucker, Steve Groce, Dale Squiers, Nancy Stewart, Missy Moylan, and Carolyn White. The hospital is led by Ted Matthews, Administrator, who is a forward thinker, and is continually expanding healthcare services in the area.

Another outstanding citizen was Mrs. Jim (Lillian) Horton. (Jim ran the tire and vulcanizing shop on E. Main with the slogan Limp In - Leap Out.) Mrs. Horton, a native of Kansas, wrote a book entitled "Mama Was Pregnant." She was the strong-arm twister of publicity, funds and encouragement of many. She'd walk in and say, somewhat like Marene, " H.V. here's what I want you to do." And we'd do it, or else. They raised money for good causes right and left.

Other special contacts were Frank and Millie Sayre. He was area manager for Texas Electric Service Company and she an artist, at one time head of the Civic League. She engineered a mass polio immunization campaign back when that was still a threat--remember the sugar cubes? With the funds of donations from that massive effort, the Club purchased a beautiful three-tiered water fountain and "arranged" to have it installed on the north side of the courthouse.

It was a beautiful thing which entailed much

sidewalk busting to provide plumbing, etc. Alas, it was a beautiful bubbling thing to behold. But later the youth discovered that putting an open bottle of dishwashing liquid in the fountain would produce an unbelievable amount of bubbles and foam which covered the sidewalk, lawns and into the streets.

It ceased to be an attraction, and was removed and stored at the City Barn for years before an auction put it in the yard of Dub Hoffmann, another well-known citizen who later was mayor, son of an early-day oil man who served as mayor during the drought of the '50s.

Marcus O'Dell later became postmaster, thanks to our endorsement of him to Congressman Omar Burleson, whose aide once asked if Marcus was in fact a Democrat. We told him that we didn't care what he was but he was the most qualified of the applicants. Marcus later led the Lions Club in a successful countywide effort to stage a vast glaucoma screening clinic with Dr. Jim Whittington, local eye doctor, in charge. (Dr. Jim later left town after an unsuccessful effort on his part to consolidate all the schools in the county (9 at that time) into one gigantic 5-A school. The vote failed in all districts. Today there are five schools in the county.

At that time I prided myself as a country editor by seeing how many local small head stories I could get on the front page. We also put obituaries on the front page then which complicated things for a long time until we moved them inside.

I will never forget the first Christmas. Our publisher Mr. Sitton hired Gaynell to help sell Greeting ads.

Back then every Tom, Dick and Harry was expected to have a greeting in the Christmas edition, which always carried Santa letters from all the kids in elementary school.

My precious memory of that season was Gaynell trooping the town on foot, door to door offering ads -- usually 2 x 4s or 5s at then maybe $5 or so, max. My memory is of her bundled in a red cloth coat against the cold and with a knit tam affair with plastic sequins all over it. She was a Christmas elf. I was so proud of her and still am.

Days in the Life

Recognizing a new editor in town, a number of employees, former patients and other citizens saw the opportunity for recruiting an ally in an on-going campaign.

The new editor hadn't been in town long before a spokesman visited and asked his help in "getting rid" of the administrator at Eastland Memorial Hospital. There were grievances that sounded well founded, but even the wet-behind-the-ears Editor realized that there probably were two sides to the story. So research with the hospital board of directors turned up a lot of information, none of which seemed sufficient for the board to fire the administrator.

The hospital had an interesting history.

An earlier hospital -- actually named the Payne and Lovett, listed in Ripley's Believe It Or Not, -- had closed when its last doctor passed. (June Bunch later opened the first nursing home in the old building.)

53

Fright Time

In later years after obits were moved inside, we received word one press day that the mother of Dr. Robert Jefferies then pastor of First Baptist Church (now First Baptist, Dallas and friend of the President), had passed away at her home in Dallas. She had visited here many times and people knew her. So we scratched our heads because the obit page had already gone to the pressroom. Finally we decided to put a small article about her death on the front page to let the public know about arrangements.

Our two were away in college: Vance in Houston and Amy in San Angelo, and we received a telephone call late one night at home. When we drowsily answered we heard a gruff voice say something to this effect: "Why did you put that woman's obituary on the front page? You didn't put my mother's there." And hung up.

That shakes one up, but it wasn't the end. Later we had another call, presumably from the same person, to this effect: "I'm going to get even with you. I know where your kids are." After we came out of shock, we tried to take precautions: had the telephone company try to trace the call, had recording devices on our phone, warned the kids and prayed we wouldn't get more calls. There may have been one or two more threatening calls, but no proof of from whom or where they came. We still wonder.

No Publicity

And then there was the city manager problem. It was a time (early '60s) when the poor City of Eastland (one of many in Texas actually in bankruptcy;

54

Eastland finally paid out) depended on parking meter receipts to buy brooms for the street and maybe pay the help. The city then was doing garbage pickup in dilapidated trucks, and when a worker failed to show up, the garbage stacked up if the manager didn't make a route. Alas, as things often happen, coins became sticky or some such, and a city commissioner came to the Editor and pleaded for no-publicity on the release of an employee's name because "he comes from a highly respected family in which there is a history of suicide. So please." Against his better judgment, the Editor complied. (Not good journalism but better human relations, lesson #31.)

The Editor got a good look at the commission side of things some years later when he was elected to that city body, and eventually was chosen mayor/chairman. In a tight-belt time, at one meeting the city manager wanted to reward some of his hard-working employees; and the commission, unwisely, approved some small raises for some on his recommendation.

Unfortunately, the manager left the meeting notes on his desk, and the police chief, first in the building each day, read them, boiled because some were rewarded with raises, but not all. He called and got a general walkout of the entire police force in sufficient force to place the city in danger.

One of the Editor's first calls, from the bank president, went like this: "Editor, we've got a problem, what are you going to do about it?" Answer: "Yes, Tom Wilson, (a special friend), I'm fully aware of it and we're working on it." The rest of the week was spent negotiating with disgruntled law enforcement and the city budget to see if we could afford to reward all employees equally. We did, they went back to work, and the banker was happy. The Editor and others didn't appreciate the walkoff, but bit the bullet.

In another city-related fiasco, the Editor, as one of five commissioners, was initially the lone standout in a city-wide endeavor. At that time the mayor, a true visionary, wanted the very best for the city and dreamed of an elaborate joint library and community center. With the encouragement of the folks of the library and of various women's clubs in town, an architect was hired; at his expense, plans drawn, bonding experts brought in, and plans moved forward to accomplish the goal of a fine, new facility that would serve the area for years.

A Vote Against

On a given meeting night all was presented in detail and all that was lacking was an affirmative vote by the commission to call an election for bonded endebtness and signatures to seal the deal. When the vote was called, all voted for an election, except the Editor. His reason: to finance the bond money necessary to build the facility would have raised the city taxes by a third. He didn't think the time was right. The brassiere sewing factory had closed and the economy just wasn't stable at that time. He too wanted the new facility but didn't think the time right.

Efforts went forward to sell the plan to the public, and members of the clubs spoke at every opportunity to encourage the passage of the project. At a Lions Club noon luncheon, one of the town's most prominent citizens was the guest speaker. Among her many other arguments in favor of the project was this: "The taxes aren't that much. In fact, because little people live in little houses, their taxes just won't be much more."

Yes, the Editor was there and wrote it down. However, before printing the article, he gave the woman who made the statement proofing privileges, and she okayed the story to be printed. The election for the facility went down in flames.

For some years, the Editor bought expensive liability insurance but eventually went barefooted. He was sued only once. It happened when an inexperienced employee, asked to go to the courthouse and record the filings of civil and criminal cases in the county and district court, which were customarily run once a month. On the day that she went was the day that the clerks had changed the order in which the various infractions were listed. Normally, the defendant was listed first; then the attorney, if any, was next; and then the offense. On that day, the attorney was listed first, the defendant second and then the offense.

So in the morning paper, one of the town's leading attorneys was listed as a second offense D.W.I. offender. The Editor's family was out of town, and he received a call from an employee asking what do we do since the lawyer called and "blessed us all out." "Print an immediate correction and apology, front page, in the next issue," was the reply, with hopes that it would all quietly go away.

It didn't; the Editor was served papers soon claiming unspecified damages, etc., etc., etc. What do you do? You go to your own friendly attorney, Virgil

Seaberry and lay it in his lap -- and worry. It costs $500.00 in fees but it was settled without costs.

On another day, a Memorial Day became ultra-memorial when a truck-train wreck near downtown sent the town into panic for days. Hazardous material was leaking from one of the many derailed tank cars, and no one could stop it. The entire downtown area was shut off for fear that there might be a horrendous explosion that could demolish the town. The newspaper people were covering the story but could not enter their downtown building. Near panic was everywhere.

Finally, a young volunteer fireman named Ken Chapman, whose business was a motorcycle shop, braved the danger, crawled under the leaking car and cut off a leaking valve that posed the danger. The debris took weeks to clean up.

That First Year

That first year on the job as the editor of a small country newspaper was the O.J.T. lab for Journalism 101 forward, and one learned more than what was being taught in classes. The textbooks didn't quite touch all the facts.

That's where you got to meet the folks, and the folks got to know your skills and limitations.

Eastland County was primarily a farming area. Raising peanuts was a $2 million crop, and farm implement dealers were prime advertisers. Industry wise, there was a brassiere factory (Hollywood-Vassarette) which hired upwards of 300 women, before the company pulled up stakes and moved manufacturing to Haiti, where the labor was cheaper.

58

The county had survived the first oil boom-bust of the '20s so was more or less prepared for the loss.

There were not a lot of jobs for men. The haydite plant north of town hired a few men. The plant baked clay into cinders which were shipped to Fort Worth where it was turned into cinder building blocks. Ranger also had a similar plant.

In nearby Cisco, there was the Boss Manufacturing Co. which turned out work gloves of many descriptions. It shut down later. Cisco's once-thriving Humble-town, a community of oil-related industry was not too slowly being phased out.

Ranger and Cisco had junior colleges, both of which had a fair- sized number of employees.

One day J. M. (Major) Cooper, the atypical A&M County Extension Agent, called up and said, "H, I'm gonna pick you up in a minute and I'm gonna show you the new hope for this county."

He took me to the Clint McCain farm south of town, just off State Highway 6. McCain, a farm loan representative, was considered one of the area's top operators. He was harvesting what is now thought to have been the first crop of coastal bermuda grass, a fast-growing, heavy-producing hay crop for animal forage.

The grass is sprigged in, irrigated if possible, cut and baled into large bales. Tractors and pickups are equipped with long spikes to handle the bales.

(At this writing, after the peanut-raising money crop ceased, when it went where the government allotments and irrigation were, coastal is the current money crop.

59

Cotton, once the big crop here and all over Texas, is now reportedly making a slow comeback.)

Also at the demonstration was E.E. McAllister, the Soil Conservation Agent, whose mantra was "The only folks interested in conservation are folks who like good food to eat, clean water to drink and fresh air to breathe."

Many farmers were at the McCain demonstration hay harvest. Clint and his nephews, John Kidd and the Brown boys, had built a fine brick home in a grove of oak trees on the 229-acre farm. Memory is that he and Mrs. McCain probably served a noon meal to the visitors, which was customary. His wife died later, and he eventually married a West Texas woman who taught school in the county. (In later years, our family visited her after Mr. McCain passed; she took a liking to our youngsters, and in time we were able to acquire the farm from her which is in our family today.)

Riding back to town after the coastal demo was another "thrill-a-minute." J.M. was nearing retirement, and his vision wasn't what it had been. (He was known as Major, and we never knew if that was part of his name or if he got the title at Texas A&M, his citadel.)

Coming off State 6 onto S. Seaman, there was a close shave.

At that time Eastland had two elementary schools: a West Ward on the far side of town and South Ward on S. Seaman St. On that day, South Ward had a portable sign (announcing something: SLOW, or PTA MEETING) which hadn't been there when we went out. Major, pretty much driving in the middle of the street anyway, was heading straight for the sign, until I hollered "Watch out!" He veered just in time. Another "J" lesson learned.

J.M. retired a little later and his replacement, DeMarquis Gordon, also from A&M, was cut of the same good cloth.

Football

The Editor is also expected to keep up with football schedules and results of the following public school teams: Seventh and Eighth Grades, Freshmen, Junior Varsity, all on Thursday afternoons and Friday nights.

The Varsity, Band, Pep Squad, and Cheerleaders -- pull out all of the stops on Friday nights, at least ten weeks unless we make the playoffs.

You'll Always Be "The Paper Man"

It didn't take too many weeks for the new Editor to realize that gathering, writing, and filling up pages for a community newspaper was a whole lot different than working for a Big Town paper where you did your beat, whipped out as many stories as possible, and then let somebody else write headlines and make up pages.

Here you check the funeral homes, cop shop, fire dept., sheriff, school supt., etc., etc., etc., yourself; make notes, find a minute and grind out as much news as possible. And that includes writing the obituaries, and listing hospital patients, but no more because of government interference.

In between times one deals with visitors, complainers, a complimenter or two, take subscription renewals, sell office supplies and/or books. Oh, by the way, make sure there's tissue in the restrooms, and that somebody or yourself sweeps out the place occasionally, and empty the wastebaskets, which stay loaded because you start your day at the post office bringing in scads of press releases, circulars, trade magazines, letters to the editor complaining about that dog leash article, and hopefully a few envelopes with checks. These you keep.

After very few weeks of misspelled names and garbled titles, as well as referring to Church of Christ ministers as pastor; you get to know that there's more to this editing than meets the eye.

By the way, was Jimmy Hughes the high school coach and Jimmy Young city manager, or was it the other way around? In time one gets it straight.

The Editor got put down hard at the first Chamber of Commerce meeting he attended. Someone casually suggested that it would be good to visit with the chambers of neighboring towns to think about putting together some kind of joint attraction. At the end of the meeting the president, a strongly opinionated attorney with a sour reputation, told the Editor in no uncertain terms he was not to mention a joint Chamber of Commerce discussion.

Much dismayed, the Editor trudged back to his office, licking his wounds, and wondering what next? He soon was visited by that attorney's brother, also an attorney of a much kinder disposition. He told the Editor not to take the other brother too seriously. "He just didn't know you too well and he was afraid of what you might write." He went on to explain that these towns were, if not actual competitors, not on the friendliest of terms. "It's Friday night mentality," he said, referring to the inner-city rivalry between the football teams, which didn't always make for peace and harmony.

That condition, existing for years and years, resulted one year in one team planting wooden crosses on the opposing team's football field. Not to be outdone, Team A members later actually dynamited the playing field of Team B. The schools wisely stopped scheduling those two teams together, and only recently have the two met on the gridirons. The Editor and the paper worked hard to lower the volumes of this old feud. There seemed to be light at the end of the tunnel, but dim.

Another traumatic football experience involving the local team and visiting team blew up world class. It happened like this: after a hard-fought key district-deciding game that had a dozen shocking plays and scores and at the end went against the visiting team, the driver of that team's bus unwisely chose to drive through town rather than going on a more direct route to the Interstate. As it passed a parking lot downtown where a group of rowdies were hanging out, someone threw a rock or something at the bus. The bus driver stopped and the entire team piled out, driver and coaches (one wielding a folding chair), and a world class dunnybrook erupted.

To add to the melee, it so happened that on that very Friday night, bank employees were moving into their brand new building directly opposite that particular parking lot. Write all that if you would. It was a classic that went through many lawsuits, trials and counter suits that cost both schools of money and prestige.

However, that event was the building season of a classic football program for the home team which won the State AA Championship a few years later, a once-in-a-lifetime writing experience for any editor.

The editor was often called on to emcee banquets and events. He did a little magic, told stories, and in his spare time, wrote.

A piece of fiction that exposes itself in idle moments:

Duel in the Shade

Meek, mild-mannered Country Editor Milford Milktoast was busy opening his morning mail, which consisted mostly of bills and solicitations, when the front door of the News office flew open with a crash and a big man barged in.

Banker Henry Hardline roared, waving a newspaper in one hand and shaking the other fist, with vengence in his eyes.

"What in the hell do you think you're doing?" were his first words, followed closely by a lengthy string of cuss words that blistered the ears of Society Editor Bessy Goodright and drew multiple gasps from Bookkeeper Louise Lassiter.

Editor Milktoast slowly got up from his chair, took off his green eye shade, and walked to the front to confront the irate visitor.

"You call yourself a newspaper man. . .you'll never get another dime of my advertising," the visitor roared.

What seems to be the problem, the editor innocently

asked.

"You know damn well, Milford. . .you ran my daughter's wedding story under that picture of the winning Hereford heifer at the county fair."

"Oh, that," the editor responded, "we caught that right after the press ran. We're going to run the right pictures and stories again next week, with an apology."

"Next week? Hell, you're going to put out an extra paper today Milford."

"Oh, we can't do that Henry, but I will extend your subscription another year to show you that we meant no harm."

"Forget it, I don't want your paper, I want revenge," he said, pointing his doubled-up fist right at the editor.

The banker pulled something from his pocket.

"He's got a gun," screamed the older woman.

"NO, NO, NO," pleaded the bookkeeper.

"Don't shoot," squealed the society editor.

Henry aimed right at the editor's chest and pulled the trigger. The gun fired with a roar. The women fainted.

The editor just stood there, shocked, but showing no blood nor pain.

Henry, wide-eyed, saw where the bullet ripped the editor's vest, and that the editor just kept standing.

Henry couldn't believe his eyes!

When he finally realized that the editor wasn't fazed, the banker fell over in a dead faint -- never to know that the bullet had penetrated the editor's packed ostomy bag where it remained embedded.

This editor also learned that obituaries that involved suicides are not necessarily musts to be included. Somewhere along the line, he has heard: "Son, it's not what you put in the paper, it's what you leave out that's important."

Another jocular bit he repeated often: "In a small town, everybody knows everything anyway, they just read the local newspaper to see who got caught."

"Into each life, some rain must fall." And for country editors, it generally comes in the form of out-of-the-ordinary human beings.

In Cisco there was a merchant, a good customer who ran a clothing store, a good advertiser but a Class A Pain in the Neck. He knew newspaper advertising helped his business, and he knew that he needed it, but he just doted on often making life miserable for those of us who called on him for his new copy.

Benny Butler was then editor of our Cisco Press. A genteel, solid old-time newspaper man of the old school. Prim and proper, a perfect gentleman always, who knew the newspaper business from front to back.

On a certain day a call came from Mr. Butler to the Eastland office and I could tell by the tone of his voice that something was terribly wrong. "I'm not going to take any more gruff off that man. . .You don't pay me enough to put up with him. . .he questioned my integrity; nobody is going to do that!"

I knew who, and I knew that Mr. B. and the merchant had had a world class clash. "I'll take care of it," I assured him.

A call to the merchant set up an appointment for the three of us for the following day at 1 p.m. And it was a nervous some 24 hours for the Publisher who knew that both of these men were dead set to have it out with each other. Both planned to be right. The publisher couldn't afford to lose a good editor or a good advertiser.

Mr. B. agreed to the meeting. I let both men explain their side: The merchant said he had marked an error on the ad proof. Mr. B. said there were no marks on the proof. Did the ad run wrong? I asked. "It was just a typo, not a price figure," the merchant admitted. It had blown over as hastily as it had begun. The two men shook hands, agreed to work together, and the Publisher drove away as his innards returned to normal.

And then there was the man in Eastland, son of a distinguished pioneer family, who apparently made up his mind to be a trouble maker for every body. He tried to tell the fire department, the police department and the newspaper how to run their business. He was a living enigma to the City Manager. He was probably a genius and had been told many times that if he used his talents for good rather than bad, that he could accomplish much. He just wanted to cause trouble.

It may have started for him some years back. He reportedly was making overtures to a married woman. Her husband found out and in no uncertain terms warned the trouble maker "if I ever catch you off your property, I will kill you."

Mr. Trouble understood, did his devilment by phone and mail, and didn't leave his home or get off his property for many years until the husband died.

However, he was able to woo and win the affection of the wife of a local minister, and she moved in with him and shared his meanness. He fell out with the church when it refused to readmit her to fellowship. She did his errands and was active in the city but apparently got fed up and eventually moved out with her son when he graduated from high school, and fled to California.

The Editor established an unstated policy of granting non-publication in the regularly printed courthouse recorded filings of teenagers, and sometimes adults, charged with first offense DWI charges, IF the charged party came to the office, shook his hand and promised never to do it again. Many have thanked him over the years for a second chance. He never grants the same privilege twice.

Country Editors are held in high esteem by all politicians because they think, mistakenly, that they'll benefit by being friends with the newspaper. And frankly editors enjoy playing the political game "from a distance." They also make money on political ads. The legendary U.S. Congressman Omar Burleson (D) was in office in the early days of the Editor's tenure, and we helped put together a whiz-bang local banquet salute the year Omar had a tough opponent.

Omar won and never forgot the help. Years later he gave the Editor's family a personal tour of the capital in D.C.

The Editor also strongly supported a young ag agent named Charles Stenholm (D) who sought that office after Omar retired. Helping in every way possible helped Charlie, who repeated and was re-elected and served nobly in Washington until the Republican-leaning Texas re-districting powers re-drew the lines which let a strong Republican from Lubbock win the new, gerrymandered district. Charlie had been begged by friends to switch parties in order to hold the seat.

He would not, holding to the LBJ philosophy of "Dancing with the one who brought me."

Locally strange things happen politically. During the early two months that the new editor worked for Onus Dick before Sitton bought the two papers, the long-time, beloved County Judge John Hart died after winning the Democratic nomination without opposition for the fall general election. A young man who had served one term in the State Legislature, having been beaten by a dashing young man who was favored throughout the district, sought the judgeship.

Scott Bailey approached the County Democratic party officials, asking for the nomination. They approved and his name was on the fall ballot. Democrats won all the races then.

Not a lot of people approved of this maneuver, including Sitton and Onus Dick, the Editor's boss. Onus Dick filed as a write-in candidate opposing Bailey. The Editor tried to remain neutral, but it was a sticky wicket. Bailey won, and proved to be one of the most outstanding county judges in the state of Texas, and at the time of his retirement, the longest-serving.

The town and the area's economy suffered two tremendous losses during the Editor's early years. One, the brassiere factory (Hollywood Vassarette), shut down. The other loss was the fizzling oil boom which played out in the 70's after once giving notice of being every bit as big or bigger than the Big one of the late '20s.

A Christmas Eve fire a block from the courthouse and just around the corner from the newspaper office on the south side of the square came very close to leveling the entire downtown. The fire departments turned out in force from all over the county and prevented what could have been a total wipeout of the town.

The Telegram crew was busy emptying the safe, hauling out subscription lists, and generally trying to save everything possible before the all clear was finally given. A generous gift was given to the fire department. Jack Graham was Chief.

It had started in an auto repair shop in the back of a dealership on S. Seaman St. The Saturday paper had been printed but the crew pitched in and with photos and prose turned out a four-page wrapper about the fire.

Auto dealership and Auto repair shop were wiped out, and the vacant lot in time became the site of the new Eastland County Newspapers Inc.'s main building in 1985.

The Editor and his wife bought the Cisco, Eastland and Ranger papers from Publisher Sitton in 1968 and continued to print the papers in Cisco, where Sitton had moved production from Ranger earlier. In 1971, thanks to federal investment credit legislation, the new owners were able to purchase a new offset press and remodel the old original Telegram building on the south side of the square into a tightly-fitted office, composing room upstairs with a dumb waiter between the floors, a complete lithographic darkroom, plate making, and the installation of the new press with great anticipation.

Operating the old hot metal plant had become outdated: buying lead and parts for the machines, and in general of printing in the old method. Offset offered so much more. Even color! Alas, it was learned later that offset also has great expenses and constant updating.

In the hot metal process, the "40-pound pigs"

chunks of lead which fed the Linotype machines, the strip-casting machines and the casting room were reusable but its volume diminished and had to be replenished, which was added cost, roughly a $1.00 a pound.

Plus molten lead was always a danger everywhere it was used. OSHA didn't exist back in those days, however. The actual handling of the trays of type and the page-sized forms had to be carried to and from the old slow four-page flatbed press. Parts for the Linotype machines were very expensive.

We just knew that we were going to save money, be able to print in color, and move into the new century with offset. We had visions of full color photographs and ads. . .my, oh, my, wouldn't that be wonderful!

BUT:

The brand new, expensive three-unit (two stacked and one down) offset press afforded us, guess what? Twelve pages. At printing speeds far beyond any thing we'd ever need with multiple, rather limited circulation runs.

The offset principle is based on the fact that oil (the ink) and water (which flowed over the plates) don't mix. The process: the image to be printed is created by photographing the "pasted up" page layouts into negatives which are "burned" onto the aluminum plates and fixed. You can read the image but you can't feel it. On the press, the ink kissed onto the impression rollers touching only the image which are in turn printable. Complicated and delicate for old hot metal printers.

And the very nature of offset called for a lot of improvements: a hoist to raise the 1,000-pound paper rolls to the top unit, an air compressor, piped water supply, expensive aluminum plates and photographic negatives (both unreusable), plate bender, offset camera and accompanying developing trays, etc., etc., In the composing room, expensive type setting equipment for straight matter and headline and ad type, photographic paper for the setters, waxers, etc., etc., etc. In addition a Little Joe to help handle paper rolls and later a forklift.

Beautiful full color photos and ads? My, oh my, yes, we did them in limited quantities and did spot (one color) in certain places. The fact is that every color used reduced the printing capacity of the press by one unit which is four pages. So our color capacity was limited with our original three unit press. We later added a fourth unit, and later two more, bringing the current total to six times four, is a 24-page capacity. They all call for blankets, rollers and constant maintenance.

And by the way, it takes expensive, skilled, experienced press operators to produce the maximum benefits.

Up to date? Yes! Savings? IF any, negligible. Ease over hot metal? Tremendous.

These presses we've always compared to freight train engines: big, heavy, and will last forever if maintained.

Many improvements are already in use today: we now go from computer screen to printed page layout without cutting and pasting. Newest twist: computer to plate; no darkroom.

Production in Eastland began in August of 1971. The editor had had a double hernia surgery in January of that year -- and later wondered if the conversion or the surgery was the most painful.

Suffice it to say that taking on the added responsibility of publishing three newspapers as well as editing made it a brand-new ballgame. The company added the Rising Star and the Baird Star later, bringing to five the number of local community newspapers to nurture.

Editing

The thing that got the Editor nearly as much notoriety as the stolen pickup episode was when he attended his first school board meeting. WOW.

E.I.S.D. board of trustees had not been regularly visited at their monthly meets so when the new Editor walked in, he was greeted warmly, but obviously with a bit of caution. He was at that time an unknown factor.

The beloved Supterintendent Wendell Siebert grew up in Eastland, had been a coach and educated himself up to the top spot at the school. His father Jesse was a popular barber in town on the west side of the square, where Shine-Man Willy Speaker was equally popular. Willy and JoJo Jones who shined on the north side of the square would later prove key to the school at a later date.

All knew him as Supt. Sieb and on that January, '63 meeting night, he had efficiently placed Hectographed (this was before copy machines) copies of the night's agenda at each place in the conference room adjacent to his office. The somewhat nervous new Editor took a look and without drawing attention, slipped the copy at his place off the table into his lap, folded it and put it into a pocket.

On the agenda were the routine: first approve bills and minutes, and then consider items including renewing lunchroom milk contracts and a number of other run-of-the-mill chores which the trustees had to accept or reject. And then these: replacing heating system boiler, consolidation, integration -- either of which, even the tyro

73

Editor recognized, could be dynamite. So he quietly settled in.

After little discussion, the trustees handled the mundane items, taking up an hour or so, and then Board Prexy M.H. Perry, local insurance man who had been a G.I. Instructor in the county following WWII, called a recess. All retired to the nearby cafeteria for peanut butter cookies, left by the lunchroom workers for their bosses, and milk, and idle good-natured kidding and gossip among the trustees.

At the end of the recess as the group began to reassemble to the meeting table, Mr. Perry thanked the Editor for coming and in a word, bid him farewell.

The young Editor who partially understood the importance of the topics to be discussed but not then protected by open meeting rules that exist today, refused to say goodbye. He didn't have much of an argument except he felt the public had a right to know what was being discussed.

The banter between Perry and Editor went on for some time, and finally, the editor pulled the sheet of agenda out of his pocket, and ticked off the items scheduled.

Still, Mr. Perry held his ground. "These are matters best discussed in privacy..." he contended.

The stubborn Editor sat back down -- expected to be bodily tossed out. Supt. Sieb said not a word. Others were quiet, so it was pretty much Perry vs. Editor.

And then Trustee Truett Gregory (the milkman who got the school milk contract), spoke up: "M.H., maybe we ought to let the boy stay." A breath of fresh air, even being called "boy."

Others chimed in, thank goodness, and Mr. Perry

saw that he was outnumbered and sat down.

The Editor then, looking directly at Mr. Perry, said, "I live here and I don't want to do anything that would hurt this school or anybody in this town. I need the town and I want to think that the town needs me. Please do not fear what might happen by my staying. I promise fairness."

We stayed into the wee hours working with the trustees on the sticky agenda items which deserved to be handled judiciously.

Consolidation was a matter that was brought forth by Eastland Physician Jim Whittington, a native son of prominence, who envisioned combining the nine school districts in the county into one giant 5A football-powerful school with new, modern facilities located in the center of the county.

He, with help, engineered the Texas passage of an incentive aid state law that would reward districts financially for combining lesser schools into more efficient large schools.

Naturally, none of the existing schools considered themselves "lesser" and had joined together to fight the possibility. However, enough citizens agreed with Dr. Jim and brought the matter to a vote.

To be accomplished, the proposition would have had to be approved in each of the nine districts. It failed in all nine, and Dr. Jim moved his practice to Fort Worth, where he was certainly more successful. His next project was an on going battle with American Medical Association about certain rules.

Later, integration became an issue because the trustees were considering building a new elementary school facility to replace two old buildings on opposite ends of the town. To get the federal assistance to build, the system was going to have to terminate its longstanding "dual education system." Blacks for years had been schooled in Douglas, a one-teacher school located a block from the square in a dilapidated frame building.

The two shiners of shoes and boots in the barber shops were instrumental in helping secure the votes of the few Negro families and the assurance to the young people that they would be accepted in the integrated system.

Both of these main stories saw ink in the local newspaper for months.

It came to pass without incident -- due in no small part, thanks to extensive local, hometown newspaper coverage.

Bored?

If lined up before a firing squad today with threat of death if giving the wrong answer to the question: Were you ever bored?

Answer: Never. Take the following for example.

On a Monday morning after a previous week in which we dealt with a public school student and his parent about some mistreatment that the student had experienced at the hand of one of the teachers, we called for a conference with the parents, the teacher, his principal and the superintendent to hear the complete story. Upshot: teacher was forced to apologize and given private admonishments about his conduct for the future.

First call to the Editor on the next Monday morning: a woman's voice and here's what she said, verbatim: "You son of a bitch, I hope you die before sunset." Now that starts a day. And of course, we learned later that it was the wife of the teacher who was taken to task.

In addition to carrying the "country cousins," which were detailed accounts of revivals, weddings, anniversaries and just plain accounts of who visited who. Other reasons for being, were the regular reports from the various women's clubs, Bible studies, and social events. The cousins were mailed or brought in, and the club events were usually brought in with these warnings: "Make sure this gets in and don't change a word."

We usually obeyed.

An interesting one in point was from a Women's Missionary Society weekly meeting reported by a saintly host, who also had a local reputation of always being late. Names will remain anonymous out of respect, but this one became a local collector's item, and we sold out of papers.

The pie`ce de la re`sistance in this meeting report was this sentence: "While Mrs. Anonymous was finishing her bath, Mr. Anonymous entertained the early arrivals in the bedroom."

Or this:

Early on the editor and his wife were invited to a local cement plant's annual barbecue, "and be sure to bring your camera."

The plant burned locally available clay, which turned the material into hard-as-rock cinders, which the parent company turned into shaped cinder construction building blocks.

After the generous feast with the employees, Plant Manager Charley Martin presided over an awards ceremony and presented Safety Certificates to those who had achieved certain "no-accidents" milestones of achievements. And we, with our trusted Polaroid, duly recorded each presentation and made notes of name, correctly spelled, number of accident-free days, etc., etc., etc., all of which were to be printed in the next week's paper.

Truly, Any-Town-USA fodder, and less than exciting.

But sometime later, maybe months, maybe years, on the occasion of being in the home of one of those earlier recipients for some reason, the Editor spotted something that proved providential.

There on the fireplace mantel in that modest but neat home was a framed newspaper photo clipping showing that man receiving his Certificate from Mr. Martin.

A place of honor for him and a wakeup call to the Editor that "this does matter."

In the early days there were often times when the young editor wondered if he had made the wrong choice. He had once considered the possibility of working for a public relations firm, traveling in high style and promoting some major company around the nation. And here he was with his new wife bogged down in a small town covering service clubs and writing obituaries. Surely there were more important things.

He decided he had made the right decision because he learned that what he was doing was important too.

It was long after the Wild West shoot-'em-up days, but the Editor one day momentarily thought it might still be on.

A local man had been killed when his car stalled on the T&P railroad tracks at one of the then un-gated crossings in town and was struck by a train, destroying the car and killing him instantly. Story and obituary duly written and printed.

Later the Editor got a call from the widow ordering him to come out to her house for a "very important story for your paper." With camera, he went, finding the grieving woman on a pull-out divan bed in the living room, amid what appeared to be dozens of full and empty prescription medicine bottles on top and around the covers where she lay.

In sobbing, halting speech she began to tell what she was going to do. A railroad man had been to her house yesterday to discuss a peaceful settlement, and he was due back tomorrow to make what he thinks is the final settlement, she said.

"But you know what?" she asked, weeping and wiping her eyes with what looked like a dirty wash cloth, "he's in for a big, big surprise."

"I'm going to kill him, just like he killed my man," and then as if to emphasize her point, she pulled a long-barreled revolver out from under the cover. It was the longest, biggest and meanest-looking the Editor had ever seen. He just hoped she wasn't planning to shoot him for running the man's story.

Screwing up as much courage as he dared, the Editor kneeled beside the roll-out bed and taking the woman's hand that didn't hold the pistol, he began to sympathize and try to console the grieving woman as best he knew how, which seemed to him, inadequate. Flying by the seat of his pants, his mind raced to think of a way to avert what could be another tragedy- -his.

In an effort to make small talk, he asked about her children. "We don't have any," she answered. "Kinfolks here?" "We don't have any." "Does anybody check on you?" "No, I'm just by myself since my man's gone." "Do you go to church, have a minister?" "I once went up there on Bassett St."

Finally, the Editor offered, "Ma'am, why don't you let me check that revolver out to make sure it's in good working order."

"Oh, I know it is," she said, "I put the bullets in it last

night after that man left."

"I know, but I could check to make sure it's in good working order for you. Let me see it, please." Slowly she handed the heavy thing to him, and it felt like a cannon to the Editor as he carefully held it away from them and eyed it as though he knew what he was doing. "You know, I've got a man who works in our office that knows all about guns. Let me take this and let him check it out for you."

"Oh, I don't know…"

"I promise to get it back to you before the sun goes down tonight."

She consented reluctantly, and he eased up off his knees, carefully holding the six-shooter away in one hand and camera in the other, carefully moved toward the door as he bid her goodbye and promised again to return with her gun.

He went straight to the sheriff's office, told Lefty Sublett the story, gave him the gun and advised him to contact the minister up on Bassett St. to go to that woman.

No printable story, but one heck of a life experience.

Newspapers are made up from two things: wood pulp and other people's business.

The Editor

By the late artist Norman Logan
80

CHAPTER 6
The Psychology of Country Editing

Some things are a given when it comes to editing/ publishing a community newspaper. One can be either a hero or a heel. Rarely is there a middle ground.

In a small town one person usually wears both hats -- editor and publisher.

And it is not strange for an editor to get into a pickle when he is just trying to cover the local news.

There are often determining factors over which one may or may not have control. Even though an editor tries very hard to be fair in all things, he recognizes that there are usually two sides to every issue. Being fair is part of the game.

But say for example, the editor covers a routine service club meeting, makes accurate notes and takes pictures of the honored guest speaker, and then writes the story and develops or sends on to the computer the best photo to the composing room. Mishaps can happen there: cutlines are switched; type is garbled; photo goes too dark or too light; and then comes the darkroom where the whole thing can be mis-shot on the camera; and then the platemaker fails to rub-up the service club story/photo properly; and then to the press where anything can happen -- a plate goes bad, ink glob onto the service club feature, water runs out and the whole plate goes dim.

And by the way, don't overlook the fact that in writing the story, the editor may have been distracted XXX number of times so the editor may have had a lapse of mind and/ or finger control and misspelled the speaker's name and assigned her some other career. No big thing, but either one of which could result in the speaker, the club president and the entire membership less than thrilled with the quality of their local newspaper. Nothing intentional; things just happen.

But then there's the day when a soul, when renewing their subscription says something like, "We sure appreciate our hometown newspaper. Keep up the good work."

81

It balances. We normally operate on the principle that if we hear nothing, everything is all right. We usually hear when things go afoul.

Requirements? A tough skin, a constant smile, and a generous portion of the acceptance of human nature.

A personal trait that might serve others: it has always been my nature to try to "complete a task" before launching another. Certainly this is not always possible, but it serves well. Because there are always interruptions which may or may not be important. However, one can and should always think ahead about what needs to be done next while actually in the process of the work at hand. To deal fairly with the public and employees is vital.

Running a Community Paper

So what does it take to run a small country newspaper? In a word answer: Patience.

In fact, the country designation has now turned into *community -- which supposedly sounds less hicky.*

The fact is that publishing/editing/running a small town newspaper calls for many unique skills. Writing soul-stirring editorials is not the lone responsibility. There are many demands.

The absolute bottom line is that there must, first of all, be a bottom line. Like all businesses, making a profit is the reason for being. One could put out the most beautiful, most newsy paper in the world, but if at the end of the month and at the end of the year, the figures show that there is more going out than coming in, then it's a failure.

Too often some in the public believe a newspaper is a public service.

There are many influencing circumstances: the ups and down of the local economy, necessary major repairs, spiraling costs of materials (ink and newsprint), postage, and a 1,001 other factors. And one must consider growing and expensive federal mandates. Postal Service grants discounts IF you follow all the rules.

Income generally comes from advertising sales, circulation and from some office supply sales. Income from circulation generally doesn't cover the cost of newsprint (which can run thousands of dollars a ton -- that's roughly two 1,000-pound rolls of newsprint, which will run several hundred papers). The bulk of the income comes from the sale of advertising -- both classifieds and space ads; and inserting pre-printed material is another major advertising plus. Legal notices are lifeblood.

There are some who are suggesting that newspapers as we know them are in their last gasps before dying completely. Commonly heard and read are such bromides as "radio couldn't kill 'em," "television couldn't," but the internet will deliver the final blow. And it is apparent that the magic of instant access to news virtually as it happens and being able to communicate and order products right off the internet screens in the current age is popular. But ink on paper has many pluses.

And nationwide (worldwide) the decline of ink-on-paper newspapers as we once knew them is a fact. The metropolitan papers have shrunk size and content. The regional papers are sometimes ghosts of their former selves. Advertising and circulation revenues have shrunk, causing major adjustments in content, delivery methods, and most drastically, vast reductions of employees.

Legal notices in newspapers are the perfect way that important public announcements are distributed and read, but being threatened. In late 2019, 25 counties in Texas had no local newspapers.

From the beginning, we've tried to treat each of the towns and areas we serve equally. There has been advantages of central ownership in savings for us, and it helps bring unity to the entire areas. Certainly there is a certain amount of jealousy among the group. Five of our papers are in Eastland County; Eastland is county seat and naturally has evolved into the strongest (at the present) retail center. That has not always been true: Cisco at one time was the trade center with more retail stores and business being done, and it is booming once again.

Associates in the trade repeatedly ask us, "Are you still running all five of those papers? Man you're crazy, why don't you just print one paper for all of them."

For a long time our answer didn't make sense business-wise, but to us we wanted to help maintain as long as possible an identity for each of the towns. It's poor economy, but it's the humanitarian thing, we believed. We waste paper every time we start and stop that press to change plates for smaller runs for the other towns, particularly for our weeklies. But we just never wanted to be the one to kill a paper for a town -- the post office has and may continue to do it, schools have and are doing it, but the little towns deserve all the help they can get.

The giant chains saw the logic in central ownership and now operate even more tightly than we ever did or could. Modern communications help make it possible; some regional newspaper pages are being designed, made up of state and national news far away in a center site, and transmitted for publication along with pages of local news.

We shuffle copy from outlying offices to a central composing room, and "common pages" (those that will run in all of our papers) are put together to join local-only pages, into newspapers, each with individual mastheads and front pages for each of our towns. It's not economical, not the most efficient, but we feel that it is fair to our entire area.

Naturally we also have asked ourselves are we contributing to the divisibility of the towns by doing this. We keep telling ourselves that we are not. They all deserve their own paper and their own identity.

Another factor: each of these towns has always been very good to us and our business.

Among the current schemes are group ownership, which provides for bulk buying power, control through central news selection and design, with content being wired to group papers around the country. The other scheme which is prevalent among virtually all papers is development of instantly accessible web pages, to which advertising is being sold and with content in variations from the print edition, plus the novelties of two-way response.

What about the web? They've been hit too, first by independents who put together web pages, usually filled with unsigned gossip, and cribbed data from the local paper and other sources, purporting to be a prime news source. Another hit for the communities is the pop- up of "free" papers distributed through racks, which strive to present themselves as newspapers, underwritten often by, you guessed it, advertising from the same local merchants who have supported local hometown newspapers for years. We always say that the distributors of "free" papers know their true worth.

These and other factors have a negative effect. Based on the old philosophy of the best defense is a strong offense, the home-towners are doubling their efforts with the staff that they have to deliver more local news, more local photographs and responsible think pieces which encourage good citizenship, safe environments and local economic growth. Often heard from the locals: "give us

Mrs. Smith hosted the Tea Club," "The Blue Jays play Podunk Saturday night," and "Billy fell off his bicycle and broke his leg."

Pure local news is the lifeblood, and as long as the hometown papers can deliver this, they surely will survive internet and other interlopers.

It behooves newcomers to the field to be innovative with ideas and improvements, which will help the locals maintain their rightful positions. There is always room for improvements, and there hopefully will always be a place for bright young people to become involved and contribute in this important information field.

The age of the instant book and the instant newspaper is upon us, but won't there always be a place for product that an individual can pick up, unfold and quietly peruse in peace?

There is this to be said: the advertising of the printed word does not grate on one's nerves or pierce one's ears as do the other kind.

Consider, at the end of a day at a computer screen, isn't it comfortable to hold a newspaper at one's own pace?

Where will the electronic media be ten years from now? Systems, hardware, software, etc., are being outdated almost instantly.

However, of the original Gutenberg Bible, printed some 550 years ago, 21 complete copies still exist today.

When one seeks recorded local history, where does one turn?

Description of Operations

Eastland County Newspapers Inc. did publish five community newspapers in the middle of Texas along I-20 between Fort Worth and Abilene.

The Cisco Press, Eastland Telegram, and Ranger

Times were published twice each week with press times on Tuesday and Friday. The Rising Star and the Baird Star published once each week, both on Wednesday.

The employees are charged with collecting news, taking photographs, selling advertising (including classified ads), and putting them in a form to be included in the newspapers. The pages are now composed on computers, and the page-size printouts are turned into negatives, which are sent by wire to an area printer press and printed, labeled and returned.

The papers are labeled, sacked, and delivered to the various post offices for delivery. Additional copies are placed in newsstands at strategic locations, with coins collected. Advertisers and subscribers are billed.

Expenses are large.

Sometimes there is profit, sometimes there is not.

The papers have good reputations for supplying the fact news and dealing honestly in the towns we serve, and we feel a responsibility to provide the best newspapers possible under less than perfect economic conditions.

Contrary to what some may think, we believe there will always be the need for a local community newspaper which help unite the citizens of a town.

Why Tidbits???

Here's a tip for would-be home town newspaper editors:

It's the title for a regular column that is very convenient for the editor to make comments about just anything on the mind-- you can usually get away with "opinions" "ideas," and maybe complaining.

A number of times I've commented on "why bananas which look so good in the grocery bins, often 'go rotten' before you get 'em home.

And some such! And you can compliment oldtimers or

pretty young girls without being considered a "mash-er".

Where did Tidbits come from?

For me: a tale remembered from youth-- about an immigrant (possibly my great-grandfather who came from the "old sod") and how he went without food for the entire passage only to arrive in the States and be told by the captain who observed that the immigrant looked so gaunt-- "Why"? he asked and was told that the poor man couldn't afford to go to the dining room.

The Captain replied, "My good man there is food down below with all kinds of 'tidbits' that you could have been nourished with.."

Moral: it pays to ask questions.

Not earth shattering, but an interesting, readable tale with a moral. And a space filler.

And then there are always compliment and gripes.

For years I've visited other churches on Sunday morning rather than my own, and written general reports, naming names and commenting on special features. It has been well-received and apparently appreciated: mention of large and small congregations and their leaders.

I've called it "Fellowshipping."

How to Write an Article

You've covered an event (emergency or otherwise), a meeting (routine or otherwise), you've been handed a press release or told of what is considered material for an article, and filled your pad with many notes. What now as you sit facing your typewriter or computer terminal?

First requirement necessary to write a newspaper article: THINK. Ask yourself what is the most important detail? How did (does) the event *affect*

88

people? Were people killed? Injured? Property damaged? What was the most important thing the speaker said? How does the meeting affect the public? What is the effect?

When you get the point of the NEWS, that's your lead. Try to get as much of the W.W.W.W. & H. (Who, Where, When, What and if possible, How) in the first paragraph.

The Civil War Pyramid

We'd been taught from Journalism 110, so just naturally assumed that it was a "Golden Tenet," handed down by Moses, not to be abused. We were taught and it was pounded into our heads that when you write an article, you put the meat and the potatoes at the top -- in the opening paragraph if possible.

Most important first, followed in descending order by less important data about the story. Well, we were taught that in making up the papers, sometimes things don't fit right, and if a printer has to cut to get it in the allotted space, the cuts are made at the bottom. That makes sense, but when did it start?

We've learned that the practice actually was a product of the Civil War. Here's why: communication techniques were primitive at best in those days, and it was possibly the war that was being covered by news sources all over the nation and maybe abroad. So a reporter in the field might be relying on a telegraph system that depended on wires strung from here to there and from there to here -- and these often were severed.

So to make sure that the biggest fact was delivered back, the writers would cram the basic facts of that day's battle or siege at the top of their communique.

Now you know.

Some (of us) compose the headline from the facts, and actually type it in first, always changeable as the process develops.

All other details of the story follow in descending order

of value.

Feature articles and puffs (chamber of commerce, etc.) can take a more casual and leisurely lead. The word to the wise now days is to try for an antidote (names of participants and how something did or will affect them.)

Quotes from participants are important to all articles.

(*Note the difference between AFFECT and EFFECT and use accordingly. AFFECT is what causes an EFFECT which is the result of an AFFECT. (The fire AFFECTED this neighborhood and the EFFECT was total destruction.)

Like It Used to Be (Slightly Altered)

We don't "write up" weddings or obituaries like we once did. Many were taken from called-in accounts, and some came handwritten through the door, all with this admonition: "Do not change a word." And we did not.

Not altogether unlike the following:

NUPTIALS UNITE

Mary Alice Swartz, John Jay
Wed In Holy Matrimony Here

In the gloriously decorated sanctuary of the Holy Emmanual Southern Baptist Church Saturday afternoon, Miss Mary Alice Swartz, daughter of Dr. and Mrs. Herman J. Swartz of Pine Crest Drive, and John Jay, son of Herman and Estelle Jay of Lot 7, Bide-a-Wee Trailer Park, were married in solemn vows.

The most Rev. J. W. Prickett presided.

Mary Alice was adorned in splendor with a snow white gown trimmed from top to bottom in chantilly lace, and trailing a 14-foot train, attached to a glamorous tiara crown encrusted in seed pearls and sparkling rhinestones, creating an unimaginable impression of pure delight.

The bride wore elevated slippers of satin-covered fine linen encrusted with sparkling multi-colored jewels.

She carried an elaborate bouquet of spring flowers, orchids, baby breath, bird of paradise, yellow plumara and lily of the valley blooms, all enmeshed with satin multi-colored fine gossamer ribbons, each one displaying gold relief emblems of quiet composure.

The groom wore black trousers and a white sport coat set off with a bright burgundy ascot. His slippers were Rockports. His boutonniere was of many splendored impatiens.

The bride's 14 attendants were each dressed alike in assorted pastel, dazzling colors, each with a giant satin bow at the busom, and strings and strings of assorted fresh water pearls and brightly colored gems with rhinestone accents. Their footwear was silver spiked 5-inch heels.

The bride was given in marriage, reluctantly, by her father.

The groom was escorted by his brother, Herman.

At the lavish reception and open bar that followed, a full course barbecue repast from Sam's Pit and Grill, served on a beautifully and lavishly decorated eight-foot serving table centered with a giant carved ice sculpture of Old Rip, the horned frog that survived 31 years in the courthouse cornerstone. Gold leaf napkins were in abundance, and the punch bowl was refilled many times. A chocolate fountain was a major attraction.

Background music was provided by Leroy Antinelly and his All Girl String Ensemble. Leroy did the vocals in his own not-to-be-duplicated style.

For her going away attire, the bride chose a seasonal bright light-weight frock in multi-colored polka dots. Crocks were her footwear. The groom chose cargos and tennies.

The couple will honeymoon at the Tides Two Motel in downtown Houston and return to set up housekeeping. He is a valet parker at the Best Western where she is desk clerk.

The parents and the preacher cleaned up the mess.

(P.S. Read Old Rip Story below.)

Messages to the Staff

Establish contacts for reports on meetings and news to be reported for our newspapers. Think your local paper first, but remember that you represent five towns so you can do your sources a lot of good by spreading their news far and wide. Chances are they'd appreciate knowing that you can get things into so many newspapers, especially if they are having a fish fry or a rodeo to which they want to sell tickets. You can help them. Recruit helpers from leaders, officers, coaches, club members, and others as well as those in charge, at City Hall, Courthouse, fire station, and police dept., D.P.S., funeral homes, clubs and organizations.

Businesses and the Chamber of Commerce appreciate being contacted and asked for news updates. We should start on these early Monday morning and ask for them to call back if things develop.

Please worry about getting other people's names into the newspaper. Journalists make notes, ask correct name spelling and write. A journalist can make stories out of very little, and we need more little stories. The big ones pretty well take care of themselves. It's the little things that our readers like to read about. Worry about our papers being relevant; we all need to worry about getting area news onto pages that run in all the papers.

What is area news? Cong. Stenholm, Rep. Jim Keffer, the courthouse, cattle market prices, taxes, Hendricks, prices, Re-Hab, West Texas Utilities, anything that affects all of us, etc.

As always, we all depend on others when questions come up that we don't know the answer to. So don't hesitate to call and ask. And when they get inquiries or requests for someone to come take a picture or pick up an ad, they shouldn't hesitate to call on others to help out. There is more to be gained by working together than trying to go it alone.

I'd like to know that every office has a routine of checking sources first thing every morning -- funeral homes, police, fire, sheriff, etc., so that we can stay on top of things. Everybody should read Mrs. Payne's stories to get a grasp of how she wraps many details into an overall story: a weather wrap-up, (flood or otherwise), a court trial, a commissioner (or any government body) meeting takes some thinking. What are the most important facts? They go at the top and everything else follows along.

Friends: A Man Named Saul

Most know me as "The Paperman" but my friend the late Saul Pullman knew me as High Voltage, a play on my initials. He was a local football hero about the time we came to town, and he went on to play for and graduate from TCU.

He later received his law degree, came home to the delight of his parents Tilly and Henry Pullman. Henry was an immigrant, and both parents, by hard work and living below their means, acquired property and wealth to leave to Saul and his sister Mozell. Saul set up practice and defended the defenseless and bedeviled the city and all with his ultra opposing views. He was a strong Democrat as were his parents before him. He helped put Ann Richards in the Governor's mansion. She rewarded him with a slot on the area Texas MHMR board, although he had no experience or knowledge of mental illness but a man of great compassion.

He was a perfect fit because he had hard-nosed rationale and sympathy for those who needed help.

We often clashed -- he was so Liberal and I tried to walk a middle ground. He ran for State Representative and District Judge, both unsuccessfully. He would have been good at either.

With relatives in the Holy Land, he visited there often and always came back with new sandals --a cousin was a leather worker.

Saul was a close friend to the Church of Christ minister, and they had long interesting discussions.

He often said to me that he knew all about Jesus -- "He is one of our boys."

Saul lost his beloved rural home in the giant New Year's Day county fire of '06.

He died suddenly, hard at work clearing brush around one of his rent houses.

Like many others we miss Saul, a good news and feature source and close friend.

His dad had been a friend and always my Rotary Club contact. The Pullman name? Henry, just off the ship, saw it on a railcar, and used it for his own name.

Scott Bailey Was a Friend and Statesman

Former County Judge Scott Bailey was everybody's friend. The Biblical "man without guile." A smile, a kind word and a hearty handshake. . . these were his hallmarks.

A man's man, Scott Bailey was a true gentleman who doffed his hat to women and stood at rigid attention for the National Anthem and expected others to do likewise.

We first knew him at Cisco (then Junior) College in the early '50s. He was, as were we, "from the country," as opposed to the "city boys." We knew that he and his good friend Blue (only name we ever heard) often hunted coons together. They followed the dogs -- and who can stand taller than that? Korea got us both. He came back for more education; he was elected to the State Legislature where he stood one term above head and shoulders for the folks in the fields and the factories.

94

We were reunited in the early '60s when this scribe was a tyro editor and Scott was appointed Democratic nominee for the office of County Judge after the death of longtime Judge John Hart.

Scott won handily against a write-in candidate and began a long and noble tenure as the chief executive officer of Eastland County.

The county had witnessed the courtship of the judge and Mary Nicholas, a Carbon native, then an employee in the County Clerk's office. It was the real thing, and their two talented offspring prove that good genes were handed down. Mary was a pillar at Cisco High School for many years, where she was affectionately known as "Mom."

Scott was true to God, his family, and himself to the benefit of residents of Eastland County. There were high times and low times during his tenure, but Scott was always Scott, "a man you could go to the well with,. ("a popular evaluation first hand from Lyndon Johnson and then Charles Stenholm.)

Counting the legacy of service and accomplishments of County Judge Scott Bailey would be like counting the stars in heaven where he now resides. As do many others, we now regret that we did not visit Scott more often during his confinement in the nursing home just to get him wound up again to tell us history as only he could. He was a historian without peer.

As we have occasionally said of others:

How do you say goodbye to a man like Scott Bailey?

Reluctantly.

Mrs. Payne

If ever there was one born to the country newspaper business, it would have to be Mrs. Travis (Viola) Payne. She was another of the many blessings bestowed on us when we needed them most. And to her last days, she was our special inspiration, critic, confidant and counselor. In her contacts and in her writing, she never missed a beat or a deadline.

She came to us through a friend who told us of her personal writings which she called "The River Road." We read a few, were impressed and started her part-time which turned into more than fulltime. She told us more than once that she wished that she had found newspapering earlier in life. A natural-born writer, a talented musician, but most of all, one of God's greatest creations and humanitarians. A devout Seventh Day Adventist, she was a true adherent, respecting all others regardless of their color, national origin or creed.

Her husband, a World War II veteran, was in failing health at the time we met her. She had an older son living in California; a daughter, married and living in Europe; and a young son at home in school. As all families do, hers evolved: her husband died; the daughter, mother of two daughters herself, came home (now remarried and a grandmother); and the younger son, with his mother's encouragement, pursued his education, receiving a doctorate degree.

Others called her Viola, but out of great respect, we never called her anything but Mrs. Payne. She wrote courthouse, crime, music, art and anything that needed writing. Everyone loved her and respected her integrity and her writing. When they wanted it done right, whether it be a wedding, family reunion, obituary, graduation or new baby, they called for Viola.

Were we jealous? Heavens no, she was our shining jewel.

As her health failed and age took its toll, she was faithful to the end. Perhaps her greatest gift to the newspaper and to the public, Mrs. Payne carefully tutored and groomed daughter Margaret to be ready to take her place at the newspaper office. And there she is today, following in her mother's footsteps and reminding us again that the Lord takes care of those of us who don't always do a very good job of taking care of ourselves.

Complete sentences. You'd do yourself a favor to read and analyze her stories. The wise learn from others. Also, we need to remember that it's good policy to let someone else read and edit our material before it's printed. What we say may make sense to us, but not always to others. Others catch errors which we all make, and ask questions which need to be answered.

Spelling counts. If you don't know how to spell it, look it up. Spell-check is not perfect. We need pride in all that we do. The pace we keep makes us run in a dead run, but we need to be accurate. You know we're judged by the stupid errors we let into the papers.

I wish, oh, how I wish, we each one could write a weekly column with names, names, names of our local people. If we could do that in every paper, we'd be more successful.

When you are out and about, be our eyes and ears -- what's new that you see? Stop, ask questions, please don't hesitate to make suggestions here at the office as to how we can increase coverage in every direction.

Benefits: one week paid sick leave and one week vacation after one year. However, we are a pretty folksy bunch, and sick children, doctor appointments, etc., are understood and provided as necessary. Salary-wise we're probably about par with the county offices.

Circulation and distribution: all papers mailed or in pay racks for above- average penetration.

We wholesale to counters and $1.00 in racks.

Production process: all type on computer; pages made up on computers. Now: Deadline: 12 p.m. Tuesday. Pages sent to printer, bundled and delivered all in Eastland County Wednesday.

We are editorially independent and try hard to give all sides equal voice. This was, as was Texas, a very Democratic County, but with the Reagan era, things changed, and now our local and state office holders are all Republicans. We repeatedly endorsed Veteran Democratic Rep. Charles Stenholm for re-election, but he was beat in the last go-round and now retired. Frankly, the Republicans think I'm a Democrat and vice versa, which is fine by me.

Major employers: EBAA Iron foundry in Eastland, a recession proof plant with employees making giant cast iron pipe connectors for water and sewer control -- worldwide customers. Eastlander Design makes hotel and hospital curtains, drapes, bedspreads, etc. . ..In Cisco, we have giant Frac-Tech Company which does exotic oil recovery and also sells large special equipment - trucks, lifts, etc. Other major employers are Cisco College and Ranger College, both in county with branches in Abilene, Brownwood, Graham. Oil play in Texas up--again. Vulcan Materials is new.

The Eastland Telegram was started in 1925 after the consolidation of a number of other local papers. Cisco Press is older as is Ranger Times, Rising Star and Baird Star and Gorman Progress.

My involvement is like this. I swept out the Cisco Press while going to junior college; the publisher realized I needed a trade so he taught me Linotype machine.

Then I went to Abilene Reporter-News while going to senior college, graduating with a BA Journalism.

Drafted in '54, out in '56, back to Reporter.

Was married one year to GayNell Ratliff when Cisco publisher called and asked if I would run one of the papers he was on a deal to buy.

I came to Eastland with my bride and became

editor of Telegram, working for previous owner for two months while deal for Eastland and Ranger was closed to join the Cisco paper. I worked for the man the Biblical seven years and wife and I were able to put together a deal to buy the three papers in 1968. We later bought Rising Star, Baird, and Gorman. We were able with "investment credit" to buy and bring the first offset press to this part of the country in '71, and operated in the original 25-by-100 building on the courthouse square. It was tight, and we designed and developed our present plant, moving into it in 1985.

Print competition: Abilene and Fort Worth came in to subscribers and news stands.

Market and changes: Ranger, Eastland and Cisco in a row on I-20 in Eastland County. Baird on I-20 in adjoining Callahan County, primarily a ranching, farm community. Eastland County was site of 1918 era oil boom (we live in one of the historic houses). So we've had ups and downs economically. Cisco was once the retail center but has lost ground, but now is coming back. Eastland is county seat so has advantage, and has recently had surge with redesign of old Walmart into a series of retails: Bealls, Shoe Department, Auto Parts, etc., but recession has slowed progress. (Under wraps are plans for expansion of a recently opened Living Center, major expansion of a materials-handling operations which does statewide highway supplies. Each of the towns has Economic Development Committees which get sales tax help to promote business. We traditionally are a tub-beater for development. Been a part of the recent renovation of an old Cisco hotel downtown, and working for the development of art center, live theater and the only appeals court museum in Texas. We have the 11th (of 14) state Appeals Court here.

Cisco has two major travel centers: Eastland has one, and the second is being built.

Vulcan is mining, crushing and delivering county's new cash crop-- Texas Highway Dept. Highway Construction Material.

NOTICE

All Letters to the Editor are subject to the following rules:

1. No personal or derogatory comments against a person or group.

2. Comments for or against policies are allowed.

3. 200 words maximum; preferably typewritten.

4. Subject to editing.

5. Signed with a telephone number and address.

6. Limited to space available.

7. We believe in freedom of speech and the rights of citizens to express opinions.

8. Opinions expressed do not necessarily reflect those of the management or staff.

9. All correspondence to this newspaper must be signed with a telephone number for verification. Names can be withheld by request, with the understanding that if asked by anyone, the names will be given.

ADDITIONAL INFORMATION

Obituaries from funeral homes only regarding the passing and services for current residents and former residents of Eastland County only.

Anniversaries, weddings, engagements, reunions and other scheduled events' announcements and reports are always welcome but are exclusively for current and former residents of Eastland County.

ARCHIVES:

Note: The items above are now charged for, a major switch for newspapers.

(Southwest Collections at Texas Tech has all our files on record.)

PRIVATE MESSAGE TO ALL EMPLOYEES, EASTLAND COUNTY NEWSPAPERS
THINK SUBSCRIPTIONS AND ADVERTISING DAY AND NIGHT!

"Nothing Happens Until Someone Sells Something"

PRIVACY: Be advised and observe that this and all information shared within these walls is private and confidential and not to be shared with anyone outside our own organization. We all must be free to share information and discuss and plan, always knowing that what is said here, will stay here. It's for everybody's benefit.

Our individual pluses and minuses are not to be discussed with anyone outside this company. I expect loyalty and honesty in every way. Everyone of us should realize that we need new advertisers and subscribers.

ECONOMY: In view of the current economic crisis that exists in all quarters, it is imperative that we all work together to increase income and reduce expenses. These measures which will be discussed will result in a better functioning operation and also hopefully preclude the need to reduce staff.

Property taxes are killing all.

In that regard, can we all consider ways to increase income; this could include each of us making opportunities to offer our services (new subscriptions and advertising) to all that we come into contact with. None of us can afford to be "specialists" -- we each should speak positively of our offerings and encourage those with whom we have contact to consider the advantages of subscribing, advertising (even if it's a classified ad). In office free time, why not try to sell a subscription? It is our obligation to put business FIRST. Cash for new unknown advertisers and credit checks to consider follow-ups.

By the same token: what we save can also be considered economic gains, so waste not. Company materials are to be used for company business. Please help with inventory reduction and making sure that expendables are wisely used. Our stocks (books, magazines, etc.) can bring in revenue if properly promoted and pushed. Can we see less visiting, more writing and selling?

HOUSEHOLD TIDINESS: We don't have enough. I am not happy with the general cleanliness of the building. I would like to see it spic and span every Monday morning: floors swept, mopped, entry clean, corners dusted. All others should be doing their part during the week helping to pick up, toss out and as best we can, maintain a clean work environment. The nature of our work is not conducive to such, I know, but we could sure do better than we are now doing. I don't expect it to happen in one day or one week, but if emphasis was placed on one area a week to spruce up, it would eventually be what we all want. Be aware of what you toss; what appear trash to you, might not be.

EDITORIALLY: I don't see enough small stuff; we put too much emphasis on THE BIG STORY, and ignore the little things. All of us can feed in minor, but important news to our readers, data that will make our papers more newsworthy. The radio station reads our copy, but they also toss in their own small items. The readers want the big and the little; a paragraph with a little head will be read. Test it. By the by, you do know that the papers are undenominational and politically independent in print, and sometimes that's hard but it's a goal we must meet. We all have our own likes and dislikes and our prejudices, but we must try to keep them from surfacing in print. Editorializing should be left to me. We want to SERVE ALL WHO READ OUR PAPERS AND BUY OUR ADVERTISING. "Fox says we report, you decide." Come up with a fitting slogan for us! -- "Fairness to all."?

HOURS REPORTS: I want everyone to report their hours, day by day, and turn them in before leaving every Thursday, adjustments made and shown for previous Friday. Hours to be held to 40 hours or less.

Also this reminder: five-day vacations are earned after one year, and may be taken in days, PROVIDED that notice is given in plenty of time so that planning can be done accordingly.

CASH, STAMP USE: Use only authorized employees to dispense gas expense, and other reimbursements from cash box. Company-related-only gas buys must turn in a receipt to bookkeeping, which should also be the only one to dispense rack coins for delivery. (Unused coins to be turned in.)

PRESS ROOM: We are all happy with the readableness of our pages and we all must work to help this continue. The Press Crew is doing a good job and has tough days ahead as we move forward.

ADVERTISING: Because we have been ultra lenient in the past, these new requirements are necessary: I want to see a weekly contact, sales report turned in with hours. Commission will be paid ONLY on those sales which are bona fied sales to NEW, not-recent customers, which was our original intent when we installed commissions. This does not include walk-ins, call-ins, unless you can convince me that you have been working on them previously. We will negotiate inserts, current and previous; making pressroom, with your cooperation, responsible in the future. Gains have been made for which we are grateful, but I'm convinced that more time could be spent on the phone to prospects and walking/driving the streets determining how advertising could help this and that new and/or longtime business and/or service. Watch for new business locally, (check city water dept.), scan area papers for sellable ads (don't duplicate copy). Credit checks, pay upfront, and check before continuing. Keep up with retiring ads to resell.

MANY WOULD-BE ADVERTISERS ARE NEVER ASKED TO ADVERTISE!

BREAKROOM: We can all pitch in and help make this common area more inviting. A CLEAN counter and table where one could have instant or bagged coffee or tea would be nice by simply boiling water. The refrigerator needs cleaning so we could use it for cold drinks, water, lunches, etc. Each of us is responsible for what we cool, use and clean up.

SHARE IDEAS: Please feel free to make suggestions to me; and I promise to listen and try to have more of a hands-on approach. ALSO: my courteous requests should also be considered instructions to be followed. Don't say it can't be done: when I started here, I wrote the news and sold the advertising for a very small salary, and it wasn't a 40-hour week either. I had loyalty then and I expect it now.

ONE LAST REQUEST: All please try to keep the on-phone and in-person casual question-askers and would be time-killers, OFF me. Put my wife through or let me know by note ASAP. If my door is closed, it should mean that I'm thinking, writing or worrying. AGE HAS PRIVILEGES! THINK ADVERTISING.

Advertising, Promotion and Inserts

(Presently pay 10% commission on NEW advertising): Responsibility for serving and maintaining relations with present advertising, and developing new accounts through active solicitation of EVERY possible advertiser in our area and border firms. Responsible for insert check-in and direction to pressroom for proper placement of inserts. Both are sales-oriented.

Bookkeeping, Label Making: Presently, Sheila Hickox. Responsible for making sure all advertising and chargeable sales are properly recorded for billing. Sends bills with tear sheets on time monthly; files monthly reports to O'Brien. Prints all labels for publications; should deliver a monthly report of all account receivables. Orders office supplies, rubber stamps, and other saleables. Subscription misses routed to her which she checks out. Also helps with postal reports.

Presently: Margaret Hetrick is currently building Eastland's page one. With the help of all parties should take the lead in helping all see the possibilities and the areas (county, cities, schools, clubs, funeral homes, new businesses, etc.) that MUST be contacted daily, regularly to make sure that we do what we're supposed to do.

Vanessa Clement sets straight matter and has a very responsible position; she does the classified page and the common inside pages which are made up of ads first that go in all the papers. She puts together the Ranger, Gorman and Rising Star pages also. Vanessa is a pretty young lady and a genuis-- at currently correcting many of my misspelled words and changes and especially at deciphering my typing, handwriting and stuttered instructions to her, converting typed (or handwritten) stories you read into the printable type. She is a specialist at designing some of your advertisements, sets headline and makes up pages-- including the classified pages.

The other male laboring in this newspaper is a key ingredient--first of all, Tommy Wells, a veteran newspaper man and now our Sports Editor. Also Stephen Forester, a truly multi-purpose person. He is ex-Sports Editor (five public schools and two colleges in the county); was Editor and designer of the Cisco Press, sports page designer, and on his own, he is also a Cisco City Commissioner. He covers Cisco College and is active in his town.

The paper is doubly blessed with Sheila and Bob Hickox. She is in charge of the important reason we are still putting out prize-winning newspapers. She keeps excellent records, does the billing, collecting and recording of the proceeds, as well as serving as central contact with the public and each of the rest of us.

Bob is the man who helps generate the reason for functioning: he's in charge of advertising, and serving five towns is a major undertaking-- fortunately he has broad shoulders and knows the area like the back of his hand. He has to; he's also the man who picks up the newspapers from the printers and distributes them to the post offices and newsstands.

Margaret Hetrick (you'll read of her elsewhere, but we just want it doubly recorded that she is a virtually duplicate of her late mother, Viola Payne). Margaret covers the south part of the county, Eastland, Ranger College, makes up pages including the very important FRONT PAGE, and she does it all-- which not only pleases us, and her readers but also is a living credit to her late mother.

Today: The Grimes Matter

For years a house on Bassett St., near downtown, and a block off State Highway 6, which runs through town, was believed by many to have been a den of illegal drug activity.

In about late '05 a new city manager came to work, and he was told that among his responsibilities was to "clean out that mess on Bassett."

106

In August, '07, a multi-law enforcement team pulled two raids on the house and found controlled substances and $8,906.67 cash and confiscated everything. J.P. Grimes, son of parents now deceased but at one time pillars at the First Baptist Church, was charged with possession for sale. A friend, J. Dool, who was a renter was also arrested, had his property seized. A tipster reportedly helped set up the raids.

Grimes and Dool spent time in jail, made bond and are free. Grimes died later.

Dool was brought to trial and after a jury was seated, was released by the judge holding that the second search warrant was improper. Most of Dool's property was returned.

In early 2011, Grimes's criminal case still had not been called, but a hearing asking that certain evidence be suppressed was held but not reported.

The authorities held an advertised public auction and sold everything, cars, house, lots and all belongings.

The two had filed federal cases asking $15,660,000.00 in damages, naming police, sheriff department, D.A., city and counties. The Abilene and New Orleans federal court denied.

Normally, it's understood that a government body is sue-proof -- unless it can be shown that the action violated a person's constitutional rights.

The Editor is trying to stay abreast of the situation, not making any comment on the guilt or innocence of the criminal charges but seriously questioning the sale of property before a conviction.

Grimes spent time and is now deceased.

What Does Being An Editor Mean?

Being the editor of any newspaper means being a booster for and keeping up with everything going on in one's area, assigning someone to get the facts, write it, with names spelled correctly, putting a headline on it and getting it into print. By the way that's a 24-hour, 7-day-a-week time frame. At a big paper one would probably work a 40-hour week, barring unforeseen ultra, extra situations, go home and live a normal life.

This is not true for a small town editor; one is always The Paper Man and considered to be on duty, at home and away, subject to being confronted with friends and strangers with tips, gripes and inquiries.

When one becomes, by whatever fate, an editor/publisher of a home town newspaper, all of the above applies -- plus automatically becoming a manufacturer, distributor, buyer at the best prices possibly of equipment and vehicles, OSHA-concerned, U.S.P.S.-complier, employee motivator/counselor, instructor/trainer, town/area booster, final authority and decision-maker about policy and legality and in your spare time, when available, you might even be able to write a column and/or a few "big" articles. You are where the buck starts and stops.

Oh, by the way, you are also expected to be a pillar in your community and worship center, an all-American patriot and the perfect family person with no negative qualities.

For people working at a newspaper -- be it large or small -- there is only one guarantee: it will never be boring; no two days are ever alike.

Every time the phone rings or someone comes through the front door, it's a brand new ball game because there's no telling what might be in store. It could mean a complaint, a crusade, a citation or whatever, and rarely, a compliment.

Who knows, they might want to buy an ad, so all are duty-bound to be welcoming with big smiles and greetings.

The Longest New Year Day Ever

Awareness to the newspaper publisher's family came as Sunday dinner was going on the table on that bright 2006 New Years's day. Multi-sirens going south on Seaman St. was the first clue; the second was the billowing black smoke seen from a south window. Maybe we'd better postpone lunch and check the farm down on Highway 6.

There we ran into another newspaper employee also checking out the smoke, which turned out to be much farther south and to the west.

About this time a veteran newswriter, who lives not too far from the smoke source, became concerned and struck out, eventually traveling the Pleasant Hill Road, only one not shut down, toward Carbon which had already been blasted on its south and west side as the wildfire swept from the Nimrod area, where it was later determined that it had started, and devoured cinder-dry grasses and brush through Long Branch, as it moved north and east. Before jumping Highway 6 at Carbon, it swept the Murray Cemetery and headed for Kokomo.

A news couple from Gorman made the trip on 6 through the smoke and emergency vehicles toward Carbon, getting photographs all along the way. Farms, homes and crops were destroyed, and at Kokomo the fire devoured an active church building. A staff photographer was traveling shooting many photos as the continued evacuees from the Lake Leon area got underway.

The southeast sky was ablaze with red flames way into the night as emergency help poured in from all directions. Many were in shelters, some still at home, and many never went to bed that night. Monday morning was a day of evaluating, (some with National Guard help) tamping out embers and still-blazing structures. It was a miracle. Key factors were public togetherness during the tragedy, and how dedicated newspeople swung into action without prompting, and the generosity and devotion of Mr. and Mrs. Jimmy Little, who opened their home for over a year for Sunday classes and worship until the Kokomo church was rebuilt.

Eastland Fireman Gregg Simmons died at the Kokomo Fire and a private airport on I-20 in Eastland County is named for him.

CHAPTER 7
The High Times...

Regardless what they say, life begins for a couple when children are born.

The new editor and his bride spent a couple of years getting established, fixing up as they could afford, the old house. It wasn't too long until the apartment rental business wasn't all that it is cracked up to be. The narrow driveway resulted in constant "she needs out, he needs in or we need out." The noise from the upstairs was not exactly condusive to harmony on the lower floor -- so in time as the rent came due, and other factors, they had the entire house to themselves. (In all, there were three major renovations, each of which was a true test of a marriage.) The house now has a Texas Historical marker. It was 100 years old in 2017.

The Editor and his wife were guests at the original opening of the Six Flags Over Texas park at Arlington. It then was mostly beautifully landscaping and a number of attractions -- Speelunkers Cave, LaSalle's Exploration, Mexican train ride, Run-Away Mine Train, etc. The park became more elaborate and certainly more appealing as the kids came along. There came a time when they were older that they did the rides and their elders made as many of the musical/comedy shows as possible, and with them later, making all the booths looking for coonskin caps, dolls and other souvenirs.

Baby Surgery

After at least one failed attempt at parenthood, in August of '63, along came a boy to be named Houston Vance O'Brien III (big mistake later in life, causing great confusion). Sure, there was doting, but after two

110

months they learned that something wasn't quite right. The doctor said hernia! Only correctable by surgery, so they submitted reluctantly. In the hospital hall as the nurses took the infant away, they overheard others commenting between themselves, "Can you believe that they are going to operate on that baby?" In spite of that, the baby, the doctor and the parents came out fine.

And so for three years there was more than average dotage, and then in February of '66, our daughter was born, putting together the "perfect" little family. She was named Amy Leigh, and what a joy she has been to this day.

The youngsters were exposed to Mrs. Green's Kindergarten, and then Vance moved into public school into the new Siebert Elementary, which had replaced two old grammar schools. So, Gaynell was able to enjoy her daughter alone for a time, and then Amy joined the public school routine. PTA, parties, sleepovers, etc., etc. They moved up to Jr. High and into high school, and that's when the fun really began. Band, plays, every imaginable diversion, Friday night football, bus trips, UIL, contests, here, there and everywhere.

In '82 Eastland stayed the season and won the State Championship Class AA; GayNell addressed Christmas cards enroute to and from the 16 games held all over the state. But isn't that the joy of having youngsters in public school.

In addition to these consuming activities were any number of reunions, family trips, the first Suburban in Eastland, to Carlsbad Caverns, the Hill Country, Monterey, Mexico, etc., etc., and finally a 27-foot travel trailer that made trips to California, Oregon, Yosemite, Cody, Wyoming, etc., etc.

On fall days, there were always excursions. As a family, the annual trip was to the State Fair of Texas, where the highlight would be either the Texas-OU football game and/or a top musical at the Music Hall.

Auto history: '54 Chevy Coup, Rambler Station Wagon, '60 Nash, '65 Ford, '49 Dodge, '68 Mustang, '70 Suburban, '76 Chrysler NY, '86 Cadillac, Vans - 2 GMC, '90 Ford Windstar, '94 Explorer, '93 Pontiac, Cadillac Sedan.

In '74 Gaynell and the Editor were invited to join a Texas Press Association tour of the Soviet Union and Europe. A friend flew them to Houston in a small plane, where they joined a People-to-People delegation of some 20 fellow scribes. There they boarded a 747 bound for Amsterdam, where they arrived the next morning. A tour of the city including the Anne Frank House, the canals, and the purpose of the tour, to visit newspapers.

At more than one giant newspaper plant, we saw Linotype operators sitting at their machines with bottles of beer handy on their tool table. "We don't do that at home," all agreed.

From the Netherlands the group flew to Lucerne, Switzerland, for a tour, of the printing industry. After touching all the Swiss attractions, the group flew to East Germany for a look behind the Iron Curtain (and the Berlin Wall). Naturally, they all got the Communist "song and dance" and were told by one of the guides, "One day we will rule the world." It took diplomacy to prevent an incident after that. Through Checkpoint Charley and into West Berlin, the group breathed joint sighs and savored the true Germany that they'd learned about in school.

And then came a flight on Interflug (they called it IF airline) to Moscow where the Intourist Dept. took charge of the group, staying at the Intourist hotel -- microphone in every room?

Here in the capitol, the Texan newspaper people received the royal treatment AND a double car load of propaganda. They were there during the midst of the Cold War. President Richard Nixon had been there the week before in his effort to thaw things; they were not melting when this group was there.

From Moscow the group went by train to Leningrad (now once again, St. Petersburg) and then flown to Kiev in the Ukraine for what amounted to a wind-down of the Soviet hardline. It was here that Gaynell lost it, emotion-wise, after so many days away from her children. She just felt so far away, even knowing that they were secure with their grandparents back in Texas. It took an Aunt Bea-type soothing by the wife of T.P.A. President Glen Seddom to make her smile again.

A last stop in Madrid was the ideal two-day rest time before the long flight back to New York, New Orleans and Houston, where the friend was waiting to fly back to Eastland.

Lydia, Where Are You Today?

She was our Soviet Intourist Guide (Guard) when a Texas Press Association People-to-People delegation toured Europe and the Soviet Union in 1974. I don't think we ever learned Lydia's last name. That's virtually 35 years ago, and we wish we knew where she is today. Then she was an attractive, young (25-30?) and to us, a dedicated party-liner. However, she accepted the gift of a New Testament from Gaynell, with whom she had become extra friendly. We'd like to think she kept and read that little Bible. Of course, we don't know because it was during the deep freeze of the Cold War between our country and the U.S.S.R.

Alexander Solzhenitsyn had just fled Moscow and we had coffee near his new haven deep inside Switzerland before we went into Russia ourselves with fear and trembling of our own. Our Dutch Guide Hank briefed and warned the some

21 in our group of the manner we were to assume once inside the U.S.S.R. We all carried trinkets (ball point pens, etc.) which we gifted to our Russian hosts, and received many, many assorted little lapel pens in exchange. At the airport we were greeted by Lydia, who would be our constant companion for days.

We were housed in the Intourist Hotel, just around the corner from the Kremlin and Gum's Dept. store. The traditional little old lady was our concierge (over-seerer) in the lobby of the upper floor where we were all billeted. We were told that she recorded our comings and goings, and of course, we assumed that our rooms were bugged, so we talked in whispers -- I don't know why; we had little knowledge that they could use. Gaynell and I ventured out the first night and looked over the walls across the River at the Kremlin (fortress); and took a quick nighttime peek at Gum -- not your average Neiman's. In the hotel, the linen was thin and the bath tissue thick. Did we feel safe? Relatively so; our two children (11 and 8) were with grandparents, far, far away in Texas.

We were given Soviet treats nightly: the ballet (not the Bolshoi which was on tour); an exciting folk musical/dance extravaganza; and then a real brain-rinsing opera, "The Huguenots" of how they were mistreated, tortured and expelled. (Babies tossed up and caught on up-turned swords!) We were wined (vodka) and dined (borsch, etc.) at the famous Moscow Arboc Cafe.

To then Leningrad we were "herded" through a midnight Moscow train station where we saw the raw and unadorned, true Russia, and boarded the Red Star Special (reportedly formerly Hitler's private train) for the overnight ride in private compartments. Hot tea was served in glasses by the traditional little old ladies.

Press Conference in White House 1977

With Jimmy at the White House

The family decided to vacation West in '76 because of all of the BIG things going on in the east, particularly in D.C., so 1977 the family planned an elaborate trip east.

Parking in Fort Worth, the four of us entrained for an overnight sit-up to Chicago on the then, as I remember, Missouri-Kansas and Texas. Between trains in the Windy City, we did one of the major museums and caught the east-bound, but in sleepable roomettes this time.

This took us first to Philadelphia, where we stayed a couple of days doing all of the historic spots, graves and all.

Then it was reboard for the final leg to the national capitol, where we arrived in what was one of the city's heaviest rain storms. After setting up in a downtown hotel and a short night's sleep, we were awakened early Saturday morning by personal escorts from the White House Army Signal Agency, which were responding to my earlier request for a modern look-see at the old place where I had worked as an Army draftee in the '50s. After a thorough tour -- from the outside -- of the old and new facilities, during which they informed that virtually all of the top-secret equipment we had used

115

before had been "deep-sixed" and that they were now the latest technology, which we did not see because my top secret security clearance had expired. They let us out downtown, where we found a McDonald's for a late breakfast and began the tours of the many walkable sites and buildings.

After 40-plus years, can't say I remember all, but be assured with a teen and a pre-teen in tow we "did them all," with stored boxes today of booklets, brochures and 35mm color slides.

In '77 (the year after the big '76 celebration) the family went by train to Chicago, Philadelphia and Washington, D.C. It was on this trip that the Editor attended a President Jimmy Carter press conference and so happened to ask the headline question:

"Was your first six months tougher than you expected, Mr. President?"

Headlines all over the nation next day, "Carter Admits That It Was Tougher."

These were indeed heady times.

We spent a number of days on the Mall at the Smithsonian and other prize locations.

On Sunday morning we taxied to Calvary Baptist Church, which several of us G.I.s had attended back in the '50s. Coincidence of coincidence. Dr. Clarence Crawford, pastor when I was there earlier, but now retired, was the visiting preacher that day. Add to that this: attending were Dr. and Mrs. Rupert Richardson, both retired from Hardin-Simmons University where he had been president during our time there, and she had taught French, which I didn't learn but needed for the B.A.

Remains of the Bicentennial celebration were still much in evidence, with souvenirs of that event still available, at reduced prices.

Another treat for us was making contact with the Don

and Mamie Martin family of Eastland, who drove up with their two children, and were staying in one of the suburbs. The two families did a lot of touring together.

For me the highlight, if not for the family, was the press conference at the White House with President Jimmy Carter.

It came about this way: before we left I wrote Press Secretary Jodie Powell stating that we were going to be there and would appreciate a special tour of the White House for the family.

We forgot about the request, but one day when we were visiting our Congressman Omar Burleson at the Capitol, we learned that there was a message for us from Powell advising that we were to be at the Executive Office Building for a press conference on a certain day at a given time.

Lunch would be provided. Wow! The timing was perfect.

So on that day and in my best double-knit and a pad in my pocket, I walked the few blocks from our hotel to the site. The Executive Office Building is adjacent to the White House and was originally the old Army-Navy building before the Pentagon. I arrived on the grounds with my letter, and was directed to the certain floor of the building, where I found a number of other newshounds waiting to see the President.

Lunch came in a brown bag served on a porch facing the West Wing. Remember this was the Jimmy (peanut farmer), "put on a sweater to save fuel," Carter Administration.

Eventually we were escorted to a conference room adjacent to the Oval office and when the President came in I observed that he, like others I know, wore his wrist watch upside down on his arm. Strange.

Don't remember much about the session, and the only question that I got in was "Mr. President, you've been in office about six months, has it been what you expected"?

Later we were given transcripts of the session, which were obviously passed on to all news sources. The Post and

Times and presumably nationwide major headlines the next morning were the AP-written article explaining that President Carter admitted being President was a tougher job than he had anticipated. (I was not named as questioner.)

Before leaving D. C., the kids asked if they could see "where Daddy used to live." We walked up Massachetts Ave. (then embassy row) to DuPont Circle, and around the corner to 21st and P St. But when we looked down 21st, we saw a multitude of mid-morning gatherings of less savory-looking residents, on virtually every doorstep of the rowed, multi-story buildings. When we lived there in the '50s, it was a peaceful, college neighborhood. We lived in the basement of a building that had a dentist's office on the first floor. It was a collegiate area. On this day, we chose not to walk down that street; remember this was the hippy-era, and it didn't look too inviting anymore. Washington was suffering like the rest of the nation.

After the lengthy Capitol experience, we reversed our entrance and trained back to Fort Worth, claimed our 1974 GMC suburban, and drove back to Eastland.

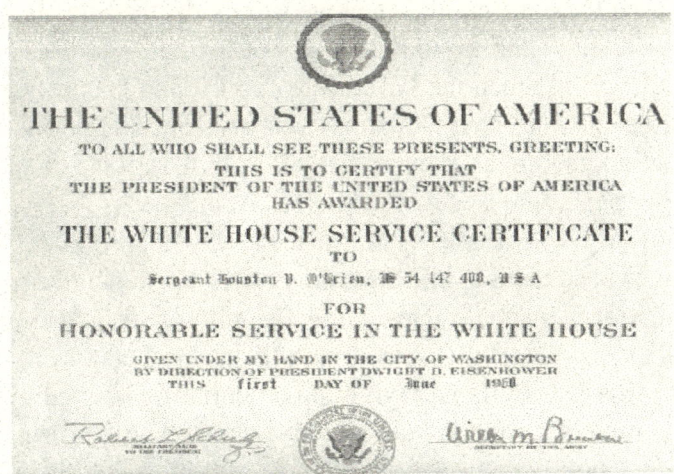

THE UNITED STATES OF AMERICA

TO ALL WHO SHALL SEE THESE PRESENTS, GREETING:

THIS IS TO CERTIFY THAT
THE PRESIDENT OF THE UNITED STATES OF AMERICA
HAS AWARDED

THE WHITE HOUSE SERVICE CERTIFICATE

TO

Sergeant Houston B. O'Brien, US 54 147 408, U S A

FOR

HONORABLE SERVICE IN THE WHITE HOUSE

GIVEN UNDER MY HAND IN THE CITY OF WASHINGTON
BY DIRECTION OF PRESIDENT DWIGHT D. EISENHOWER
THIS   first   DAY OF   June   1958

On Newspapers
By Frances Marshall

Newspapers have been printed in the world for almost three hundred years. The first one, according to history, was called a "broadside" and was a single sheet printed on one side. Its name: "Presentation of New English Affairs." Its purpose, "to prevent false reports." Published by Samuel Green in Cambridge, Massachusetts, in 1689.

Sunday's Chicago Tribune was printed on presses bigger than a freight train, on paper especially made from trees grown on the Tribune's own property in Quebec, brought here on their own boats. The newspaper owns its own TV station, influences the thinking of millions, and under the direction of the late Colonel Robert McCormick, was one of the most controversial newspapers in the world. The Sunday paper weighs pounds, takes hours to read. Full-color pages spark up advertising through the paper, lithographed like a Christmas card, and the "funny paper" section has only two or three features for a "child." All the rest are highly spiced and dramatized serial stories for adults, featuring love, death, crime and the big jokes of married life, business world, and the Army.

It used to be different. When we were kids, the Sunday edition after Thanksgiving ran pages of toy ads, and used a little red and green ink. Even as a kid, I found that very exciting - a signal that Christmas was coming. The paper was, of course, much thinner, but not as thin as grandpa's evening paper, the German language "Abenpost."

Newspapers had a long life in those days. Everybody we knew used them to line the pantry shelves, after cutting scallops or V-shaped edges along the side of the paper. All dresser drawers were lined with them. Mothers never scrubbed a floor without laying out an entire Sunday edition to protect it from the kid's muddy shoes. The grocery man fringed sheets of newspaper and stuck it on his screen door, so that it moved and shooed away the flies when the door was opened and closed. When babies were born at home (and they usually were), the doctor asked for stacks of newspapers. (I read somewhere that due to the ink, papers were fairly sterile, if still unopened and untouched.)

Anything that had to be wrapped around the house was wrapped in newspaper. We covered our schoolbooks with it, wrapped the garbage up in it, tried to train generations of dogs on it. Paused to put a thick layer of it over the cake of ice in the ice box, to make it last longer. Mama made the gingham dresses she spent the summers in by whacking a pattern out of newspaper.

Kids had two ways of making money on newspapers. One was to have a paper route, which meant being up at dawn to deliver the papers before school, and the other was to sell the accumulated papers to the "Racksolyrom" man. I was 16 years old before I knew that meant "Rags, Old Iron!" We called him by the phonetic name above, and he bought stacks of newspapers for real pennies.

Now, almost everything we used newspapers for has a special product made just for that purpose. They actually make and sell "Garbage Bags!" I think there's still one place left where the newspaper is unreplaced -- people still have to train dogs.

Interesting is the names of newspapers, a list that would be new to many, and a few thumbnail sketches on their history. The names of great newspapers are exciting in themselves - the London Times, Memphis Press-Scimitar, Toledo Blade, Manchester Guardian,

New Orleans Times-Picayune, San Francisco Chronicle -
they conjure up images of far-off places.

CHAPTER 8
The Low Times

The first Empty Nest sensation came probably in the fall of 1985 after we deposited Amy at Angelo State University in San Angelo, where she had elected to study after a year at Hardin-Simmons University in Abilene. Big factor was that her longtime beau Mike Woolley was also in his upper years as a student there.

Gaynell and the Editor had driven from Houston to Angelo after depositing Vance in Favro Hall at the University of Texas Medical School and getting him squared away in his first year of medical training. Amy had pretty much taken herself and her belongings to San Angelo, so the parents spent a few days with her there getting her established, and then headed home -- sans children to Eastland.

That first year was relatively calm, but as with all things, subject to change. The Amy-Mike romance cooled, and the grades too. In Houston it was a successful first year, and he was chosen for research work at M.D. Anderson for the summer session, so elected to stay there.

Amy came home to actually accomplish college credits at Cisco Junior College. Vance entered his second year at Med School and time rolled on.

In the spring of that school year, things began to fall apart. He had been recommended for taking a break from school. With his determination and Irish stubbornness, he absolutely refused to even consider it. Also Baylor G.S. biochemistry followed.

The parents hoped for the best and returned home, only to be informed by a medical school official in a telephone call that Vance wasn't going to be able to do term exams. Thus began the beginning of the end of medical school and a crushing blow for a son's hope

122

and dreams of being a physician/researcher Ph.D.

He applied for research employment at the University of Texas in San Antonio. The job worked well as he performed in that lab. Still study-hungry, he was taking courses, and giving up the job, set himself for Master's degree at that school.

Somewhere in the middle of this of summer, an HSU friend of Amy's invited her to go with her and his family to Cancun, Mexico, for an outing. Mother was reluctant, and father is forever haunted by consenting.

On that excursion Amy met an OU ROTC graduate who was there with his parents -- and the spark was struck. At home we heard, "He's the grandest guy. From a family makeup so much like ours, same church, same values, etc., etc., etc." By this time she had accumulated credits at CJC and moved to Tarleton State University in Stephenville, 40 miles south of Eastland. There she found counselors and supporters who helped her move toward a degree in the customary four years.

And so it evolved, wedding plans were announced.

All of this was extremely hard on Gaynell, and it wasn't doing the old man any good as plans were mapped for a June wedding with all the trappings: showers, dress selections, invitations, receptions, etc.

But it came to pass and the newly married couple headed for Ft. Polk, Louisiana, for his first duty station. Parents nursed their personal wounds, as did Vance as he manfully gave it all his best shot.

Christmas, '86 proved good. The kids came and we all put together the best time possible. Amy landed an Extension Office job and brought pine saplings from that tree-growing area to be planted at home. In 2010, they are now higher than the two-story house.

Their assignments after Polk included Fort Sill, Oklahoma, closer to home to us and his parents in Oklahoma City. Later assignments sent them to Hawaii where he had his first command and where their first son Levi was born, and to begin the climb up the promotion ladder. An assignment to Nashville,Tennessee, earned him a master's degree and then to Monterey, California, for Italian language.

Next came an assignment to Santa Marinela, Italy, where he attended Italian Military Academy and their second son Luke was born -- and still his rank rose. The next assignment to a National Guard Unit near Oklahoma City and their daughter, Laura Leigh was born. While the Army family was living in Chandler, east of Oklahoma City, where he was heading up the National Guard Unit, Amy was able to complete work for her master's degree at Oklahoma State University in Stillwater. Next assignment to Washington, D.C. where their next daughter, Leigha Noel was born. Another assignment to Rome where he worked in the American Embassy as did Amy, whose Family-Relations degree put her working for the State Department as Community Liaison.

Next came a tour at the Pentagon in D.C. Amy worked for the Department of Navy as a family analyst. Unknown to us the marriage was failing.

Retirement time for him was drawing near, and the family had looked forward to a retirement location on the Texas Gulf Coast, as Amy hoped that "things" might get better. On trips to Texas, they found Port Aransas and staked it out as their retirement hope. He could have retired as a Lt. Colonel.

Amy decided to make the move. She applied and was immediately hired as the Extension Agent at Aransas County. She packed the over-priced Cadillac Escalade deluxe wagon and came to Texas -- to find housing for her and the kids and for her to go to work. He was to finish his tour and join them, she thought.

He was offered promotion to full colonel and an

assignment at the Embassy in Rome.

He accepted the eagle and the job and at a high impact promotion ceremony, praised Amy to high heaven with tears in his eyes about how she had helped get him where he was.

Back in Texas after the ceremony she was enjoying and performing in her new positions. The kids loved the small shore town where they could be typical American kids.

Divorce came.

So, what's the situation at the beginning of the 21st century?

There's still The Editor and Gaynell, co-publishers, and there is still Eastland County Newspapers, Inc.

And oh, yes, grandchildren -- Levi born in Hawaii, Luke in Rome, Laura Leigh in Oklahoma City and Leigha Noel in Washington, D.C.

Vance is a big helper to the not-so-young-any-more parents at the newspaper.

As all could imagine, this all has taken its toll on parents who have always been concerned for and about their children, the business and the welfare of the communities they serve.

There have been many comments over the years from fellow newshounds that they envied those of us who were able to acquire and operate freely newspapers of our own rather than laboring for others.

Fun! You should live so long, and don't say it can't happen.

The COLD light of morning was the theme of a Dallas Methodist minister's recent Sunday TV sermon as he used the story of Jacob's awakening to learn that he had been tricked by Leaman, and given Leah to wed, and not his intended beloved Rachel, in exchange for whom he had worked seven long years.

So what did he do? He worked seven more years to

get Rachel. Message? When things don't turn out as planned, one just keeps on keeping on.

And for many in times of weather, financial, personal and national panic, things certainly are not working out to the satisfaction of many.

And on most every corner one sees real stick-to-it attitudes; just everybody and every entity is re-thinking many things; cutting back, learning to do without and just keeping on, keeping on. We all do it at our homes, in our work places, and especially in our businesses.

And there's a plus here too: we're all learning that some things we can't do without, like faithful employees and good business practices, but extra help and some frills we thought we couldn't do without, are finding that a lot of things are possible when we put our minds to it. Wonder if this would work on the national level, the state level, county, city? At this particular time could there be things that could be put on hold for the time being? Are there not conveniences and maybe even services offered that could be trimmed? We see dedicated efforts in some areas and zero in others. We all are seeing trimmings in many areas that we once thought untouchable. If asked to save money and stay within budgets, what would you cut on the national level? State level? County? Your city? We all can think of many things.

Editing Highs and Lows

As a guest of the Navy, a visit to the famous aircraft carrier Lexington, then a training center at Pensacola, Florida, was a definite high. It is now a major historical museum treasure permanently moored at Corpus Christi. When the Editor visited, it was being used to train pilots and crews to fly onto and off these giant marvels.

Our host was the Naval Air Reserve unit at Grand Prairie, which invited a dozen or so Texans to fly down for the visit. Among the "shipmates" was Bailey Marshall, the first executive director of the Texas UIL.

We roomed in the crew quarters, were served in the mess center and hosted by the brass for tours, lectures and upfront viewing of the exciting and dangerous flight onto and off the busy decks. We met the young pilots, sat in their cockpits, and glowed with pride at their skills.

We later were given permission to invite locals for the same experience: the late T.M. Fullen, Bruce Pipkin and Marcus O'Dell had the same experiences. The perk was good for many articles and photos, all extolling praise for the Navy.

And the Low Side

There was the Steve Benefield affair.

He was a local Ranger product who returned to set up an empire of trucking, buying and selling businesses and generally making a big splash, hiring, wheeling and dealing.

Unfortunately, as it evolved, his dealing included suspected trafficking in the illegal controlled substance industry. The law worked frantically to bring him down, but he time and again eluded the efforts.

How were we involved? One of our employees was married to a Ranger policeman, who may have been working both sides of the fence as a close associate of Benefield. So the papers were in a way a condiut; we learned things, and possibly were being used. After one failed attempt to pin him down, an ad appeared in our papers (without our advance knowledge) that read something like "You missed me. Signed Steve."

Because of the high incidence of illegal drug trafficking at that time, a number of concerned citizens from throughout the county joined together and formed an organization known as PADD, Parents Against Dangerous Drugs. Attorney Mike Siebert, Joe Cooper of Cisco, Gorman Police Chief Cecil Funderburgh (later to become Eastland

127

Police Chief), Texas Ranger Gene Kea, then-Sheriff Don Underwood, D.P.S. official Jerry Mathews and other law personnel were actively meeting, offering rewards for tips, and trying desperately to bring down the drug traffic. Certainly the newspapers were heavily involved with scads of publicity, and all would like to think that good came of the many efforts.

After he was successfully brought down, a local lawman bought an ad that read "What goes around Steve, comes around."

Before he was found guilty, we had a long letter from him (now in our files) attesting to his innocence. Virgil Seaberry, our longtime trusted attorney friend, shown a copy of the letter, wondered why Steve's attorney permitted it to be sent, and suggested we not print it, as badly as we wanted to. It would have sold a lot of newspapers.

Another crime incident of note: the town was plagued at one time with the repeated rapes of older women. Here also, citizens banned together, meeting, offering rewards and working to help lawmen find the culprit.

At one updating meeting of note with a room full of people, the editor asked if there were any suspects and/ or persons of interest? One of the lawmen, obviously without thinking, blurted back: "As it stands right now, even you haven't been eliminated." Furious, the editor started rising from his chair to respond in kind and or to leave the meeting -- only to have Attorney Seaberry sitting in the next chair, calmly place his hand on the Editor's shoulder and push him down. (The unthinking officer, now retired, later asked for my vote when he was running for county judge, and learned of how offended I had been at his comment.)

Incident after incident: a disgruntled husband, upset that the courts had given his ex-wife everything in a nasty divorce, calmly walked into the courthouse where she was an employee, and shot her in the hallway. She later died of her wounds. The editor had just left the courthouse which was just across the street from the paper, lucky not to have been a witness. The shooter had been an avid hunter and the paper had taken many trophy photos of his kills over the years, but not this one.

He was found guilty.

Every time that phone rings or someone walks in that front door...

And How Does It End?

Kind reader, if you've stayed this long in this, then you deserve to know "the rest of the story."

It isn't pretty and only proves the adage "Into each life, rain does fall." And like the one-time popular song, "too much has fallen on mine." Not just me, but the family's. What first appears as the golden career, family, business, status, etc., etc., is not always without road bumps along the way.

As stated, in the 1980s multicolored clouds appeared. A dark one was a diagnosis of son Vance; a bright one, at the time, was the elaborate wedding of daughter Amy.

And today is an important key in the family organization.

Also after 20 some years, that glamorous military marriage came to an end in a nasty divorce matter.

Thanks to her personal tenacity Amy now has a life she cherishes: her two sons and her two daughters, a protective, caring husband, Jon, our Precinct Justice of the Peace, a home, a future and enjoyment of a simple life back home.

Parents NEVER cease to be parents, so Gaynell and I have weathered these crises, seemingly unending, but are thankful for each other, children and grandchildren, a successful business, a home and property.

Facilities, supplies, location, all keys -- but the greatest of all are the dedicated employees who start on time, do whatever needs to be done and stay until all that can be done is done.

This Country-Publisher has been blessed with some of the best, and alas, some of the worst. And naming all of over 50+ years would be impossible because in addition to the two extremes listed, there have been literally hundreds who have come and gone, moved on for whatever reason.

But the ones who come to mind stand out like beacons.

Ted Rogers was the printer I first met in 1949. He was a younger old school printer who came back to the shop where I had just been hired as a printer's devil (which meant that I was expected to do everything everybody else didn't want to do.) Ted helped me in so many ways to learn, and we became good friends. Lo and behold before this tale is spun, we turn out to be kinfolks.

He cast "cuts" with molten lead using cardboard molds to make the few illustrations used back in those days. He took the cuts and with type, built ads to go into pages with machine-set type along with the handset headline type which he set letter by letter. He then hefted the heavy pages onto the old eight-page flatbed duplex press, after he had loaded the press with 500-pound rolls of newsprint. Then he printed the paper, usually six or eight pages; two runs were necessary if more than eight. To get ready for the next day's run, he killed out the pages -- tossing the type and casts, but not the quality individual letters making up headlines and big type in ads. To "kill out" meant to toss all the lead back into hell boxes to be remelted and reused. It was hot, heavy and tiring work. That in a paragraph was "hot metal" printing which was the norm for many, many years.

He was a bachelor, was the last person to reside in the Cisco Mobley now Hilton Center, across the street from the Cisco Press plant. His folks, whom he visited often, lived in Santo.

As we advanced in skills (?), moved away and then back to work the seven years for Publisher Sitton, we continued to work with and befriend Ted. After we acquired the three papers, he naturally was a vital cog in the operation, and we would have never made it without him.

And it evolved that we made the move to "cold type" -- that is offset printing of the papers, and Ted made the transition from hot type to offset -- probably one of the few in the nation of the old-time printers who were able to do that. Most were too set in their ways; Ted was set, but he realized that his work would be easier. He would not have lasted in the old system.

Did I mention that he could have a short fuse? More than once I stopped him from decking a bumbling helper who would not take instructions. But he never used a bad word, nor told an off-color joke. He loved horses and children in that order. His big fault? Doing himself rather than teaching and expecting others to do things.

And then as we progress, he and Gaynell's mother fell in love, and were married and he became a truly happy man, who took her family as part of his own.

Everybody who worked with Ted or knew him, loved him, and it was a sad day at his passing. He was newspaper and family.

* * *

Gary Slade came to us from the pressroom in nearby Breckenridge after he had suffered a hernia surgery. His talents far exceeded the press room. For us he was a good writer, a photographer and at the most crucial time, when our high school football team was bound for the State Championship, Gary was the man who wrote, photographed and covered the team as it deserved to be covered. He knew the game, players, coaches -- and move on he did. First as quality controller for the production of USA Today at the Arlington plant; and later as founder and publisher of the highly successful niche international trade journal ENTERTAINMENT TODAY, which is the Bible read world-wide by all the people in the park and entertainment business. We're always glad to say he came into his own with us.

And there have been the losers. Chief among them was a pressroom supervisor who bit off more than he and we could chew. He walked out leaving a printing contract unfulfilled.

A trusted office manager/editor in one of our towns -- stole us blind on cash subscriptions, etc. Confronted, she admitted that hers had been the best job in town. She and her husband signed notes; she died and he paid for a while. Chalk it up to being too trusting on our part.

One year we had a valued, trusted employee walk off on a press-deliver night because the person I had put in charge was asking him specific questions about his job.

You try to be fair; you can see when some are not giving 100%; I've always expected my polite requests and suggestions to be taken as orders without shouting it out. A beloved city manager once told me long ago when I had suggested that he should be tougher on his employees: "Oh, H. I've found that in the long run, I can get more done with a kind voice." Of course he was right.

To be un-named here doesn't mean that one is unappreciated. I'm not getting paid by the word.

There Will Be Bumps in the Road

On Tuesday morning before Christmas, which was a Saturday in 2010, the editor got an early haircut and the editor was in the emergency room at Hendrick Medical Center in Abilene before it got good dark. The redundant colon had struck again -- this time with a vigilance. Three previous attacks had been "resolved" mechanically and locally, by good ole Doc Simpson, but this one was not to be an easy candidate.

Fortunately the colon specialist with whom we'd had colonoscopies for years was on duty that night and came to check me on the gurney on which I had waited for hours -- in misery, I might add. He put it bluntly -- we can fix it or you can die. When can we fix it? I'll put you in a room, give you some sleep help, and see if I can arrange an operating room for morning.

Next thing I knew I had "been there and done that" and was in a room with extra plumbing attached to my chest. The doctor had said many times before that if we could do this on a schedule there would be no bag. If you're not prepped, there will be, he would add. I wasn't, and there was. During the several days there I was being trained to maintain, change and keep sanitary with the extra facility. Toward the last day when the poor aides were doing the dirty work as I learned, late one night one said after the unpleasant task, "Thank the Lord, this is my last night on this floor. I'm transferring to the blood unit."

Recognizing the situation: my coming home from the hospital and her mother not doing well at home, daughter Amy saw the need and came immediately. We all had planned a great Christmas together, and she and the grandchildren did an outstanding job of celebrating the holiday as best as they patiently could between my hospital bed and Gaynell's home bed.

Amy brought me home after a week, and with home health assistance I recuperated, gained strength and weight, and slowly learned to accept my new limitations.

But Gaynell's condition worsened, and after a trip to the

local hospital, she too was bound for Hendrick where she had tests, a stint and tender loving care. Upon release she was dispatched to a rehabilitation center, which proved to be a fiasco of an experience. Brought home, she actually was in worse shape than when she went to Hendrick.

On a given night with Vance and I upstairs, and she in the downstairs bedroom because of her extended total discomfort, she took too much, the wrong combination, both or whatever. Fortunately Vance heard her gasping for breath, went to her, called me and neither of us could rouse her from what appeared to be a deep coma. "911" -- total response from all departments as well as the good neighbor, physician Dr. Hazelip. Gaynell was taken to the local emergency room where Dr. Way advised us later that night or early morning that he was going to put a breathing tube in and that we should begin notifying next of kin. It was that serious. Only call went to Amy in Port Aransas where she had returned to her family and job.

We had to move her to a facility which has long-term breathing help the local doctor said. Hendrick had no spare critical care bed available; Regional did not answer their phones; Harris in Fort Worth? Go for it! And she was put on a helicopter. Vance and I ran home, packed, toothbrushes, etc.; and headed to Fort Worth, not knowing what to expect.

We found her swaddled in tubes, still in a coma and totally unresponsive. Amy drove up and arrived about 5 o'clock, as unknowing as us. The staff was super but noncommittal -- don't think they knew what to expect either. We stayed late, found rooms reasonably close, and continued the wait. About Thursday Gaynell began to rouse; she recognized Amy, and apparently partially knew what she had narrowly escaped. It wasn't until the early part of the next week before they released her; they needed her room. We brought her home.

Eventually, all except her, agreed that she needed extensive skilled nursing care and she was checked in, not without a hassle, to the local nursing facility. She mended, gained strength and weight, had a tremor and not totally mobile but alert with a sharp memory.

Our local physician who checks both of us suggested that we leave her in the facility where she was safe, comfortable and being well cared for, especially if I plan to have my colon system returned to normal, which was an option and which all urged me to do.

Presently I cope. It's not the most desirable routine.

Gaynell is home and I am almost sound.

The blessing out of all this is that Amy and Jon and the children have moved back to Eastland and are happy at the farm out on Highway 6 (the Carbon highway.) They recognized the need to help look after me and Gaynell as well as assume great responsibilities at the newspaper where they are fitting in beautifully.

As of today Levi graduated from TCU in 2016. Donna (Jon's daughter) from Sul Ross in 2018. Laura Leigh is finishing at Cisco College, Leigha started Texas Tech, and Luke is in Underwater Diving Training in Houston.

Meanwhile Vance and I spend quality time with Gaynell. She and I are closer psychologically than we have ever been. There is time now. Previously I was too busy with the business which is time-consuming, and she with the financial/records responsibilities as well as home, children and grandchildren concerns.

In due time, things come around.

As It Was, Is and Will Be

The year 2011 was a bummer for many of us. Thank goodness it's looking much better today.

Gaynell's general health had been in decline for some time with fluctuating blood pressures, and let's face it, years do take their toll. We mildly marked our 50th wedding anniversary in 2010, kept our heads above water, with the home and the business pretty much on auto-pilot as the world took nose dives and cart wheels.

After a number of medical ups and downs through 2011, the editor played the Grinch and virtually stole Christmas, with an emergency surgery. All turned out okay, if not hunky-dory, at least satisfactory, alas with extra plumbing.

During the recuperation, it all caught up with overly concerned Gaynell, and she took a physical dive, developing pneumonia, a stay in intensive care, and finally a safe return. All except her decided she needed continued skilled nursing, which she has had, and is making great progress daily.

That all pretty much sounds like a downer, but as in all things, there are silver linings. It all prompted miracles.

Our daughter Amy, her husband and children responded in the hours of need. They came during all the trying times, bolstering and helping Vance who lives here and has always been a part of the team. Together they all helped put things to right.

And it has evolved even richer. The parent's needs they saw very clearly, which helped them make the final decision to move to Eastland, which we had all talked about many times, but it just had never gotten done.

Amy and Jon gave up positions and their home, all of which they loved on the Texas Coast, to relocate to Eastland and help parents and the business.

They are living at the farm which they are updating; the children loved the Eastland schools; and now they all wish they had done it sooner, and continue to be a part of this newspaper.

Jon and Amy are fitting right in. With their children's help, they raised and the kids showed 4-H hogs, goats, and chickens, and they plan to put in a garden soon. Jon has filled all the freezers with deer meat taken from the farm pastures and is raising cows and growing hay. Jon was elected JP 1 in 2018. Amy plans to keep the newspaper alive as long as she breathes, just like her Daddy.

To make a long story shorter-- they are the answers to prayer and are taking a tremendous load off the shoulders of the Country Editor. Amy has been named County Extension Agent, and with their fresh views, innovative ideas and energy, they are also kicking Eastland County Newspapers into the 21st Century, website and all. What blessings. The super big plus: the business stays in the family.

After what seemed for a while like a long, dark tunnel, the Old Folks are now thinking about that long-hoped-for return trip back to Big Bend, and who knows, maybe even Ireland when the stars are lined up.

There are smiles. There are memories: all kinds, the good and the not-so good:

The Saturday after a pressday long ago when I pulled a blind-drunk Linotype operator, who had not contributed one line of type all day, out from under his machine and fired him.

The time I had to explain to a losing candidate because we had not delivered his paid-in-advance inserts two days before the election. His check had cleared. He threatened to whip me, but thought better of it.

The Christmas Eve firemen who put out the fire that threatened the entire town as we emptied the safe of mailing lists, records and accounts receivables.

The day, I gave an honoree a wilted corsage which had belonged to another woman at a banquet because the florist had not delivered the one that had been ordered.

The time at a meeting I introduced a state representative like this: "And now for a man who needs no introduction, he won't get one."

The banquet at which we had arranged for Cong. Charles Stenholm, guest speaker, to take a surprise telephone call publicly from his wife back in Washington. We gave him an original Jan Herring painting, and his dilemma as he tried to describe it to her and on the provided phone where they were going to put it in their townhouse was amusing.

The night I had to give the invitation at the conclusion of a Billy Graham film shown to a full house at the Majestic Theater. I don't remember if any responded. The plaque presented by an admiring coach with my name misspelled. They never knew.

A $25 check from the Chicago Tribune for a story called in about a teenager who had flown a plane from there to Eastland.

The horrible night the pressman got his hand caught between press rollers. He first was taken to E.M.H., then flown to Hendrick and right on to Dallas.

High time: named recipient of the Texas Good Law Enforcement Award for a series of articles on the backlog of criminal cases in 91st District Court. Check $250.00 (big then) and a plaque presented by Atty. Gen. Waggoner Carr in Austin.

As military writer a visit to NORAD headquarters; Vandenberg AFB Space Center; General Dynamics research center; and A.F. Academy.

The joy of the victory by Incumbent Cong. Omar Burleson over his toughest opponent after we had sponsored a fund-raising salute in Eastland on behalf of his race. Years later on a family visit to D.C. and him at the Capitol, he thanked our family before an entire committee hearing he was participating in.

The night Gaynell and I stayed up most of the night in the little compartment on the Red Star train from Moscow to then Leningrad, drinking hot tea in glasses made by the little ladies who served with toothless smiles to us non-communists.

The 1982 Eastland Football State Championship won at Baylor Stadium.

The horror we witnessed the night we boarded that train in one of the Moscow stations. We had been told by our guide to keep our eyes straight ahead. Why? Because there was every kind of degradation one can imagine going on openly by desperate men and women, drinking and doing everything imaginable to each other, as in Dante's Inferno? Our eyeballs were singed.

We always taught: the national news magazines capsule the world once a week, surely we can do Eastland County once a week.

Deadlines: anticipated -- 5 p.m. Monday

Boring? I wouldn't trade it for a speckled pup.

Country Hometown newspapering -- that's where the fun is, and done right, it's a ministry to fellow humans.

Be It Recorded

Although this book has the Editor's name upfront, it should be remembered that development and operation of the newspaper business described herein was not a "one-man" event. The corporate documents of EASTLAND COUNTY NEWSPAPERS, INC., carries the names of H.V. and Gaynell O'Brien. It is true that H.V. is the "glad-hander, man-about-town, meeting attender, ad salesman and type-writer pounder; it was for many years that Gaynell was the at-home record keeper, check writer, bank balance balancer, meal deliverer, children trainer, etc., as well as being the beloved partner in this operation.

Other contributing participants included son Vance, who today as this is written is Number One care-giver for his mother who is wheel-chair confined.

Amy, the other family member who was involved with the newspaper over the years now, with her husband Jon (one of our special family gifts) committed to carrying on the "news history" with the newspaper.

They are the "plan" for the future.

The Old Rip Report
(Added by special request)

Due to the seemingly unending recall and writing about one of Eastland County's most famous celebrity -- a frog, the Editor has been publicly labeled the unofficial, unpaid old Rip ultra-promoter. He has been honored repeatedly by the Chamber of Commerce and other sources to "re-tell the Old Rip story."

And here it is:

History has recorded that in the year 1897, on the occasion of preparing the cornerstone for a new Eastland County Courthouse to replace one that had burned down. A time capsule was planned.

Of course, the usual Bible, copies of the local newspaper, and maybe a pint of Four Roses, as well as photos, names of elected officials, etc., etc., a group of young teenagers--as often happens-- thought it would be a hoot to slip a horned toad into the virtually sacred corner stone.

(Now a horned toad is a mean-looking, but harmless ground toad (frog) common then to this entire area. Drastically reduced in number today because of pesticides and habitat reutilization and other causes, the horned toads are few and far between today.

Custom named the "frog in the tomb." Old Rip's name was suggested by the Washington Irving short story, "Rip Van Winkle, " about a man who supposedly took a long, long nap.

Climax to the Old Rip Story-- years later, in 1928, the cornerstone depository was open upon the occasion of setting in a new one for the present court house...

...and, low and behold, as the Methodist minister was ceremonially taking out the ancient relics, he picked up the toad -- and the toad "twitched"-- he was still alive; alive after 31 years.WOW! What a legend, no, not a legend, "gospel truth."

Or so it has been told throughout modern Eastland history.

He toured and at the Whitehouse President Calvin Coolidge is quoted as saying "Well, I'll be."

Old Rip has been named the official State of Texas Horned Toad and is celebrated annually with recognition here, there and everywhere-- even a grand exhibit appearance at Six Flags Amusement Park. (Embalmed, Old Rip can be seen today in his casket in the lobby of the Courthouse.)

The editor has been honored repeatedly to re-tell the Old Rip TRUE, SWEAR-IT-ON-A-BIBLE story of Old Rip who slept peacefully in the cornerstone.

We wrote the official book on "Old Rip" available at eastlandcountytoday.com or ecn@att.net

THE TRUE STORY
OF

**The Texas Horn Toad
That Slept 31 Years In The
Eastland County Courthouse**

BY H.V. O'BRIEN

$13.00
includes postage
& mail

eastlandcountytoday@gmail.com
1201 S. Seaman Eastland, TX 76448

POSTSCRIPT

As might be imagined this effort has been a long-time a'borning-- so where does it stand at the beginning of 2020?

Many-blessed to still be active at age 88, you can imagine this re-telling is a scattered collection of many scribbled rough-typed sheets, in and out of a tattered briefcase to be worked on, re-done, added to and taken away from, so heaven only knows what the finally-finished product may be.

Hopefully of inspiration and encouragement to any and all who might be interested in how it was done and could be done again now by all of "word-consciousness," ambition and determination.

A string of what some might see as dumb luck this humble scribe sees as divine guidance. And so would recommend that whosoever seeks whatsoever, would be encouraged to search for, find and follow the same Director that has always been and is available today.

Enjoy following the path of this humble word-merchant.

One friend called him Scoop.

Some who disagreed with his philosophy of freedom of the press or whose names were unintentionally misspelled, called him names not appropriately used here.

But the greatest rewards of all were to be called "friend."

Today:

2020-- County-wide print and digital publication of Eastland County Today, incorporating the five community mastheads into a larger once a week publication.

Print, digital, live website, social media presence, serving scads of readers eyes regularly.

eastlandcountytoday.com

Thank you, Eastland County, Texas
H.V. O'Brien
ecn@att.net or
eastlandcountytoday@gmail.com
website: eastlandcountytoday.com

GAYNELL O'BRIEN　　　**H.V. O'BRIEN**

There Will Always Be The Need for the Hometown Newspaper

It has been a team effort from the day that Gaynell and I said "I do." She has been the inspiration, motivation and the stimulation to help bring it all about.

As a trait of my family and upbringing, I'd be more likely to just go along and get along as things happen. Whereas Gaynell's family trait has always been "get it done now," possibly due to their raw West Texas, sand storm-enduring heritage.

So much of that enthusiasm and push has certainly been stimuli for us both to strive on with positive attitudes that "it can be done."

Certainly there are many others who have inspired, cajoled and pushed along the way.

Are there ever truly "self-made men'?

John Bright (1811-1889) in the only Bartlett quote on the subject, said:

"Benjamin Disraeli is a self-made man and worships his creator." So perhaps the Christian heritage of both of our families had a bearing on helping bring about "The Making."

Steadfastness to moral mores may have been a major factor.

Also from Bartlett:

"He noblest lives and noblest dies who make and keeps his self-made laws." -- Sir Richard Frances Burton (1821-1890).

Ours was a shared responsibility: she with bookkeeping, bank statement balancing and general financial skills, kept us out of the poor house. Mine were the out-front confrontations with the public in our world as well as regretfully often late-night coverage of meetings, rallies and events, which too often left her alone to get the kids to bed and keep the house going.

So it was a team effort, and perhaps should be titled "The Joint Making" of a hometown newspaper.